Why Tutoring?

Other Books by Author

Success in School and Career: Common Core Standards in Language Arts K–5

Transforming Early Learners into Superb Readers: Promoting Literacy at School, at Home, and within the Community

Why Tutoring?

A Way to Achieve Success in School

Andrea M. Nelson-Royes

ROWMAN & LITTLEFIELD
Lanham • Boulder • New York • London

Published by Rowman & Littlefield
A wholly owned subsidiary of The Rowman & Littlefield Publishing Group, Inc.
4501 Forbes Boulevard, Suite 200, Lanham, Maryland 20706
www.rowman.com

Unit A, Whitacre Mews, 26-34 Stannary Street, London SE11 4AB

Copyright © 2015 by Andrea M. Nelson-Royes

All rights reserved. No part of this book may be reproduced in any form or by any electronic or mechanical means, including information storage and retrieval systems, without written permission from the publisher, except by a reviewer who may quote passages in a review.

British Library Cataloguing in Publication Information Available

Library of Congress Cataloging-in-Publication Data

Nelson-Royes, Andrea M., 1964-
Why tutoring? : a way to achieve success in school / Andrea M. Nelson-Royes.
pages cm
Includes bibliographical references and index.
ISBN 978-1-4758-0747-9 (cloth) -- ISBN 978-1-4758-0748-6 (pbk.) -- ISBN 978-1-4758-0749-3 (electronic)
1. Tutors and tutoring. I. Title.
LC41.N45 2015
371.39'4--dc23
2014048616

Contents

Acknowledgments	vii
Foreword	ix
Preface	xiii
Introduction	1
1 Centuries of Tutoring and Its Impact on Student Academic Success	7
2 Evaluation of Tutoring Programs	29
3 Successful Tutoring Programs	61
4 Technology and Online Tutoring	93
5 Student Motivation and Parental Involvement in Tutoring	125
Appendices	151
References	167
Index	181
About the Author	191

Acknowledgments

I would like to thank my husband and children for their continual support. Special thanks to my editor, Bobbie Christmas, at Zebra Communications. I also want to say thank you to Karen Woodward, EdM, founding director, Tutoring Partnership for Academic Excellence and senior program director, Saint Paul Public Schools Foundation; Kara Bixby, MPP, director of research and evaluation, Saint Paul Public Schools Foundation; and Kait Steele, director of field operations and strategy, 826 National. The information provided from these individuals on best-practice tutoring programs enriched this book. Also, special gratitude to Jack Goodman, founder and chief executive officer of Tutoring Australasia, for his expert perspective on international homework assistance/online tutoring programs. A sincere thanks to all.

Foreword

I needed my first tutor during my junior year in high school because I was not a good mathematics student. I scored a 275 on the mathematics section of the Scholastic Aptitude Test (SAT) and was worried about getting into college. My school assigned me a professional mathematics tutor. He was a stodgy, socially awkward man with poor hygiene; however, my tutor was knowledgeable, tough, and exceptionally patient. After two months of receiving tutoring, I scored 400 on the SAT exam. A 400 was not a great score, but it helped me get into a good school, Wesleyan University.

As an individual who has been tutored and the chief executive officer of 826 National, I know firsthand the difference tutoring can make in a student's life. At 826 National creative-writing and tutoring centers, there are more than six thousand volunteer tutors who work with students daily. Many students that come to our centers do not have access to individualized attention outside of 826 National.

The time students spend with a tutor who works with them on their schoolwork is priceless. It sets students on a path to academic success. Tutor training is vital because many students look to their tutors for help with their schoolwork. For students to have the best experience possible, tutors must also make the tutoring experience pleasurable. Continual evaluation of tutoring programs also ensures that the tutoring experience is optimal for both the student and tutor. In our 826 National programs, it is evident that both students and tutors benefit from the tutoring experience.

Why Tutoring? A Way to Achieve Success in School reveals the answers to some of the questions 826 National has explored for more than a decade:

- What makes a successful tutoring program?
- What motivates students and tutors to participate for years?
- What is the best way to evaluate and determine successful programs?

Tutoring is an integral part of students' academic success, whether it occurs in an after-school program or some other method. Tutoring provides much-needed support to increase educational outcomes for students, especially for students who require additional assistance for twenty-first-century academic and lifelong success.

Dr. Nelson-Royes's thorough research takes the reader on a journey through the history and theory of tutoring, from its beginning centuries ago to its role as a twenty-first-century learning device. Tutoring plays a pivotal role throughout history, and Nelson-Royes demonstrates that tutoring makes learners better students and sheds light on what 826 National has explored for more than a decade.

Why Tutoring? A Way to Achieve Success in School can be a resource for stakeholders to use to understand the importance of tutoring in the education landscape and the community. With its practical information supported by research and theory, I trust this book will help stakeholders achieve their goals in tutoring. Assessing whether tutoring helps students thrive is a first step to support students on the road to success in school and beyond. I commend Dr. Nelson-Royes for her contribution to a very important subject.

Gerald Richards
Chief Executive Officer, 826 National

Preface

Education attainment is more important to our nation's economic success than ever before. Over the past decade, our nation's students' low test scores on standardized tests have alarmed many stakeholders. Students have not demonstrated mastery of basic reading and mathematics skills. With numerous students lacking basic skills in reading, mathematics, and writing, additional assistance, such as tutoring, is vital. Tutoring must therefore continue to be available to help students achieve academic success, especially students at risk for academic failure.

In 2001, the enactment of the No Child Left Behind Act led to remarkable opportunities for numerous students to obtain tutoring to improve their academic achievement. The latest change—the Common Core State Standards—demands that our nation's students achieve success in the global society of the twenty-first century. The Common Core State Standards are the result of a state-led initiative to establish common educational standards in English language arts and mathematics across public schools in the United States (Common Core State Standards Initiative, 2010).

The Common Core State Standards are rigorous, designed to be pertinent to the real world, and reflect the knowledge and skills that students need for success in both college and career. Students will undoubtedly need support as they develop strategies to approach increasingly complex literacy skills. Many students will benefit from well-planned tutoring programs that specifically target their areas of academic weaknesses.

Higher-paying jobs require more education than minimum-wage jobs. As a result, individuals with only a high school diploma find it increasingly difficult to enter the middle-class rank in America. According to the National Center for Education Statistics (2013), total undergraduate enrollment in degree-granting postsecondary institutions increased by 37 percent in the most recent decade, from 13.2 million students in fall 2000 to 17.6 million in fall 2009. Between 2011 and 2021, undergraduate enrollment is expected to increase to 20.3 million students. By 2018, about 62 percent of jobs in the United States will require some postsecondary education (Carnevale et al., 2010).

Accompanying increased enrollments is an equivalent increase in students who lack college preparation in basic skills such as English and mathematics. In 2011, the National Center for Education, the primary federal entity for collecting and analyzing data related to education, revealed that numerous students leave high school without the advanced reading and writing skills they need to succeed in college and a career. According to the Alliance for Excellent Education (2011), every year an estimated 1.2 million American high school students simply drop out of school.

Although tutoring is not obligatory, it is an essential tool to enhance students' academic accomplishment. Not every student needs tutoring, but all students can benefit from it. Even the most advanced students can profit from a supportive tutoring relationship that rewards them for their undertakings and inspires them to superior achievement. All students must achieve academic triumph to ensure their success throughout school, college, and beyond. Tutoring keeps students on track and allows those who are falling behind to progress.

Why Tutoring? A Way to Achieve Success in School examines tutoring as a practical strategy to achieve academic success. When implemented judiciously, tutoring affords every student the opportunity for a meaningful education. According to a Chinese proverb, "Tell me, and I will forget. Show me, and I may remember. Involve me, and I will understand." Many tutored students will find this Chinese proverb personally truthful.

Introduction

In the past decade, national attention has focused on the achievements of our nation's students in school. Calls for accountability, criticism of failing schools, worries about low standardized test scores, and a shift toward greater emphasis on teaching and learning have dominated the discussion of education in America. Today the Common Core State Standards that demand that our nation's students achieve success in the global competitive economy have resulted in a significant impact on education, and numerous schools continue to encounter diverse instructional shifts.

Tutoring is a viable strategy to provide supplementary instruction to increase educational yield, especially for students who require additional assistance for twenty-first-century academic and lifelong success. The main purpose of tutoring is to make needed provisions for students to attain essential knowledge and skills for academic achievement. Tutoring is also an excellent way to spend time with needy students. The additional assistance decreases the frustration that often results from their lack of understanding. Furthermore, tutoring is an effective approach to building the skills, study habits, determination, and confidence students need to improve their learning ability.

Tutoring is used across a number of academic domains and age groups and at all levels of schooling, including homeschooling, remedial programs, and special education programs, as a way of helping struggling students. According to Sullivan (2011), high school students are the fastest growing group of consumers using tutoring, because of competition for college admission.

Not every student needs tutoring, but when tutoring is necessary, it greatly contributes to a student's academic accomplishment. Even exceptionally capable and highly motivated students often use tutors. Tutoring as a form of instruction is used worldwide, and its effectiveness as an instructional method has been documented extensively. Research suggests that tutoring helps students become more organized, self-assured, and proficient at identifying relationships between ideas. More importantly, students develop higher-level cognitive skills that enable them to understand and express complex ideas. Some researchers have referred to tutoring as the gold standard for effective instruction.

In 2007, Gordon et al. defined tutoring as one person who provides individuals, or small groups of students, academic instruction to reinforce what they are learning in the classroom. Tutors may be adult volunteers, peers, homework hotlines, teachers, franchised learning centers, clinics, or private institutions. Generally, tutoring programs are classified by methods of instruction (individual, group, or online), instructional goals (advancement and remedial), and the sources of finance (public or private) for learners. Although tutors may have several students they work with, in groups or separately, they are defined by the acts of one-on-one communication they provide to students.

Why Tutoring? A Way to Achieve Success in School offers educators, school administrators, policymakers, parents, caregivers, and community members a practical and research-driven perspective on tutoring that links theories, research, and practice. The book examines tutoring as a viable strategy to increase academic success in education. In addition, it provides readers with information on establishing tutoring programs within educational institutions or ventures outside formal education, such as after-school study programs. It is a resource that provides stakeholders with an effective educational strategy that helps them meet the demands of twenty-first-century learning challenges and enhance the academic achievement of all students.

In this book, stakeholders will find the answers to the following questions and more:

- Why use tutoring?
- Why are meaningful evaluations needed in tutoring programs?
- What are the different types of evaluation models?
- Why use online tutoring systems?
- Why are student motivation and parental involvement vital in the tutoring process?

This book is organized into five chapters, as follows:

Chapter 1, "Centuries of Tutoring and Its Impact on Student Academic Success," focuses on the history of tutoring, tutoring and the No Child Left Behind Act, theories of learning, constructivism, the purpose and benefits of tutoring programs, and tutoring formats.

Chapter 2, "Evaluation of Tutoring Programs," explains evaluation standards, types of evaluation, the program evaluation process, the importance and purposes of evaluation, and the role of evaluation in education. The chapter ends with a discussion of some common evaluation models and approaches that can be used in tutoring programs, including connoisseurship, objective-based, goal-free, adversary and judicial, Kirkpatrick's four-level, and Stufflebeam's Context, Input, Process, and Product (CIPP).

Chapter 3, "Successful Tutoring Programs," discusses tutoring and interpersonal relationships and the effective components of successful tutoring programs. It provides a list of the core essentials for tutors in successful tutoring programs too. The chapter ends with highlighting the Reading Recovery tutoring program and three best-practices tutoring programs in the United States.

Chapter 4, "Technology and Online Tutoring," discusses the technology of interactive learning and the Net Generation, along with an overview of online tutoring. The chapter also provides a practical example of a prominent United States–based online tutoring organization, Smarthinking, Incorporated. In addition, it focuses on SRI International, Worcester Polytechnic Institute, and the University of Maine, institutions charged with the evaluation of the effectiveness of online mathematics tutoring. Further, the chapter highlights two international online tutoring institutions—Tutoring Australasia (core service, Yourtutor), Australia-based; and Tutor-Vista, India-based. The chapter ends with a list of some of the major private global tutoring companies covered in a report by the Global Industry Analysts Incorporated, a leading publisher of market research worldwide.

Chapter 5, "Student Motivation and Parental Involvement in Tutoring," looks at student motivation and the importance of motivational factors in tutoring. In addition, it focuses on the significance as well as the best practices for parental involvement. The chapter also highlights the National Parent Association and Family Engagement in Education Act and ends with final thoughts on tutoring.

Each chapter ends with Points to Remember, a section that summarizes the topic. The appendices include the Joint Committee on Standards for Educational Evaluation: Program evaluation standards statements; a list of the Saint Paul Public Schools best practices for tutoring programs; as well as resources for engaging parents in education.

Tutoring provides the knowledge and skills that prepare students for success in the complex and ever-changing world of the twenty-first century. Most stakeholders who employ tutoring believe that the investment in tutoring advances the academic standing of students in the short term and the level of academic attainment in the long term.

Chapter One

Centuries of Tutoring and Its Impact on Student Academic Success

This chapter focuses on the history of tutoring, tutoring and the No Child Left Behind Act, theories of learning, constructivism, the purpose and benefits of tutoring programs, and tutoring formats.

HISTORY OF TUTORING

The word tutor is derived from the Latin *tueri* and originally meant "one who protects, guards, and cares for" (Rapoport et al., 1989, p. 16). This definition highlights the duality of the tutoring relationship and its particular significance. In the ideal situation, a tutor is committed not only to meeting specific academic goals, but also to creating a personal connection of trust and caring. Rapoport et al. further states that the tutoring relationship combines task-oriented training with the affective elements of friendship.

For the purposes of this book, tutoring refers to any program that helps students understand and acquire the knowledge necessary to complete assignments from a regular classroom. An educator, a paraprofessional, another student, a volunteer, or an online tutor can deliver the instruction, as long as it promotes independence and empowerment. Tutoring is one of the oldest forms of teaching methods and has been around longer that the common form of instruction that schools provide today.

The story of tutoring began in early civilization, with the transmission of knowledge through oral tradition. Tutoring was essential for survival of the individual and the culture of the tribe, and parents recited folklore to tutor their children by showing them how to practice life skills. Parents tutored their children, for example, when they taught their children how to make a fire or hunt. The long history of education reveals that parents have often provided one-on-one instruction in the form of tutoring.

During the times of philosophers Plato and Socrates, select students were tutored at the Academy in Athens. Plato taught at the Academy, the first institution of higher learning in the Western world. Plato's famous student Aristotle, who also became a philosopher, was one such student, and he studied at the Academy for twenty years.

During the Middle Ages, the children of nobles and the wealthy received their education from tutors individually or in small groups. Similarly, children from less wealthy families often became apprentices to learn a craft or skill from a master, another one-on-one form of teaching. These forms of tutoring were used throughout Europe and other Eastern civilizations, even before the seventeenth century. The current formal educational system evolved from those early forms of tutoring.

S. Alexander Rippa (1997) described tutors of early America as teachers who taught Latin, grammar, arithmetic, English, and Euclidean geometry to the sons of aristocratic plantation owners in the southern colonies. During the late eighteenth and early nineteenth centuries in America, parents often arranged private education for their children. These undertakings were especially popular in elite southern families. Tutoring arrangements were highly informal well into the twentieth century. In one-room schoolhouses, children of varying ages, abilities, and grade levels were educated together.

In the North, schools—rather than private tutors—were more common, both in the colonial and early republic eras. Colonial New England towns often pooled resources to create common schools. In these institutions children were provided with the language skills necessary for reading the Bible, subsequently encouraging moral order in communities. Northern states organized teaching much more systematically in the early nineteenth century, as public schools became the norm and tutoring declined in significance. Nonetheless, tutors still existed in elite families in the South and North in late eighteenth- and early nineteenth-century America.

Research indicates that the South relied on tutors more and longer than the North. Settlements in the South were more scattered, which made it more difficult to establish schools for children. As a result, tutors became a vital part of the education of these children. Southerners did not develop the same fondness for public funding of economic development that northerners had. Northerners believed that education spurred economic progress and social stability, but in the agricultural and stratified South, only the elite could spare the labor of their children. Consequently, private education with a tutor became the privilege of those living on larger plantations.

Generally young men, and sometimes women who were unmarried or had not established an occupation, fulfilled the roles of tutors for wealthy families. Southerners often employed young northern men as tutors, since the North educated a much larger share of its population. For example, Eli Whitney (1765–1825), best known as the inventor of the cotton gin, worked as a tutor for a family in Georgia shortly after he graduated from Yale University.

Tutors continued to play a significant role in teaching as more formalized educational institutions became available. In many well-known colleges, such as Oxford and Cambridge, tutors lived in the residence halls with students. These living arrangements continued as colleges were developed in the United States.

Today, tutoring continues to be an effective strategy that helps students succeed academically and places them on a pathway to academic and lifelong success. Tutoring, once a privilege afforded only to the children of the wealthy, is now commonly accessible through schools, colleges, universities, libraries, churches, community agencies, and public and private tutoring institutions. In some countries, tutoring is a parallel education sector that provides supplementary instruction to students.

TUTORING AND THE NO CHILD LEFT BEHIND ACT

In the United States, the growing significance of tutoring was augmented by the No Child Left Behind (NCLB) Act of 2001. The NCLB was publicized as the most extensive bipartisan education legislation that Congress ever passed. The NCLB provides funding and supplementary educational services (SES) to students in "failing schools," often in the form of tutoring. In the United States, the NCLB mandated that schools ensure all students pass state proficiency exams in reading and mathematics by the 2013–2014 academic year. This has not happened, however, and many students still struggle to pass state proficiency exams.

Under the NCLB Act, districts receiving Title I funds are required to offer free tutoring and other supplemental educational services to students from low-income families who attend a Title I school. The proposed use of supplemental services has increased schools' and parents' interest in tutoring. District school personnel may be asked to help parents select a provider from a state-approved list.

Title I refers to the largest single program of the Elementary and Secondary Education Act (ESEA) of 1965. The ESEA was a federal law that provided guidelines for education in kindergarten through high school. The act also contains provisions that deal specifically with ensuring that all children have a fair, equal, and significant opportunity to obtain a high-quality education and reach proficiency on challenging state assessments.

Title I schools are those that do not achieve Adequate Yearly Progress (AYP) for at least three years. AYP refers to an individual state's measure of yearly progress toward achieving state academic standards. AYP is a minimum level of improvement that states, school districts, and schools must achieve each year.

After the NCLB became law, companies and tutoring groups rushed to be part of the new industry. As a result, many private tutoring institutions capitalized on the tutoring industry, and the tutoring industry grew as one of the first steps toward institutionalized tutoring. Many tutoring institutions inform parents and caregivers that public schools may be responsible to offer students tutoring services, if the schools are unable to meet a child's academic needs.

According to Steve Pines, executive director of the Education Industry Association (EIA), spending on tutors has increased more than 5 percent a year (Sullivan, 2010). The EIA, founded in 1990, is an advocacy group that promotes the education business in pre-kindergarten through grade-twelve markets. The EIA is the nation's leading trade association that represents more than 300 fast-developing and diverse organizations. These organizations serve families, communities, and schools. Many tutoring and learning centers are members.

Michael Sandler, founder of the education research firm Eduventures, estimated the size of the tutoring industry at $5 billion to $7 billion a year (Sullivan 2011). This amount is ten times greater than it was in the year 2001 after the passing of the NCLB. Eduventures has for two decades been a consulting firm for university leaders, colleges, and education-industry providers. It is also the industry leader in research, data, consulting, and advisory services for the higher education community.

Although the NCLB was publicized as the most extensive bipartisan education legislation, many people have criticized it. Congress has attempted for several years to overhaul NCLB. On March 13, 2010, President Obama's administration released "A Blueprint for Reform: The Reauthorization of the Elementary and Secondary Education Act." In addition to seeking an overhaul of the NCLB Act, "A Blueprint for Reform" challenges the nation to embrace education standards that put America on a pathway to global leadership.

The Common Core State Standards, the new wind of change, demand more rigor. The demand will present challenges for some students, especially students from "failing schools" and some who have demonstrated low standardized test scores. The Common Core State Standards will therefore force many institutions of learning to readdress how teachers teach and how students learn.

THEORIES OF LEARNING

In 2007, Gall, Gall, and Borg in *Educational Research: An Introduction* defined the term *theory* as an explanation of a certain set of observed phenomena in terms of a system of constructs and laws that relate these constructs to each other. Put simply, a theory is a combination of factors or variables woven together in an effort to explain whatever the theory is about.

In general, theories based on scientific evidence are considered more valid than theories based on opinion or personal or anecdotal experience. Individuals must be thoughtful when comparing the appropriateness of theories. Operating from a theory provides guidance as to how various strategies or operations are expected to work. Additionally, a theory provides order and consistency to what is to be accomplished.

Today it is essential to provide the justification and documentation of the theoretical base that supports new instruction. Many contemporary federal programs in kindergarten through grade twelve under the NCLB (2001), including reading, supplementary educational services such as tutoring, and special education, require that instructional practices and reform models be scientifically based as a condition for funding.

Educational researchers have completed many studies about factors that influence and predict students' success in school and beyond. Many studies identify interventions or factors that can be transformed into interventions to improve students' academic accomplishment.

Jere Brophy (2001) devised a list of the combinations of intervention-oriented research on basic features of good teaching. Brophy's list of effective interventions was derived from empirical research on teaching practices associated with improvements in student outcomes. Brophy's synthesis of research reveals that educational researchers and theorists have discovered many effective interventions for improving students' academic achievement.

Table 1.1 shows Educational Researchers' Identification of Generic Features of Good Teaching.

Table 1.1. Educational Researchers' Identification of Generic Features of Good Teaching

- Supportive classroom climate—Students learn best within cohesive and caring learning environments.
- Opportunity to learn—Students learn more when most of the available time is allocated to curriculum-related activities and the classroom management system emphasizes maintaining students' engagement in these activities.
- Curricular alignment—All components of the curriculum are aligned to create a cohesive program for accomplishing instructional purposes and goals.
- Establishing learning orientations—Educators can prepare students for learning by providing an initial structure to clarify intended outcomes and cue desired learning strategies.
- Coherent content—To facilitate meaningful learning and retention, content is explained clearly and developed with emphasis on its structure and connections.
- Thoughtful discourse—Questions are planned to engage students in sustained discourse structured around powerful ideas.
- Practice and application activities—Students need sufficient opportunities to practice and apply what they are learning and to receive improvement-oriented feedback.
- Scaffolding students' task engagement—The educator provides whatever assistance students need to enable them to engage in learning activities productively.
- Strategy teaching—The educator models and instructs students in learning and self-regulation strategies.
- Cooperative learning—Students often benefit from working in pairs or small groups to construct understandings or help one another master skills.
- Goal-oriented assessment—The educator uses a variety of formal and informal assessment methods to monitor progress toward learning goals.
- Achievement expectations—The educator establishes and follows through on appropriate expectations for learning outcomes.

Source: Based on research findings reported in: Brophy, J. E. (2001). Introduction. In J. Brophy (ed.), *Advances in research on teaching 8*, 1–23. Oxford: JA1 Elsevier.

In education and psychology, learning is commonly defined as a process that brings together cognitive, emotional, and environmental influences and experiences. These influences and experiences acquire, enrich, or affect change in one's knowledge, skills, values, and world views (Illeris, 2002; Ormerod, 1995). Learning as a process focuses on what happens when the learning takes place. Consequently, explanations of what happens constitute learning theories. A learning theory is a conceptual framework that describes how information is absorbed, processed, and retained in the process of learning.

Learning is one of the most important human activities. Learning is at the core of the educational process, although most of what people learn occurs outside of school. For centuries, philosophers, psychologists, and great thinkers have sought to understand the nature of learning, how it occurs, and how one person can influence the learning of another through teaching and similar endeavors. In the late nineteenth century, research methods were systematically applied to collect scientific evidence about learning.

Epistemology is the branch of philosophy that studies the nature of knowledge and the process through which knowledge is acquired and validated. The drawings from various epistemologies have resulted in several prominent theories of learning. Learning theory is descriptive and explains and predicts how individuals learn. Theories of learning and instructions for practice should go together.

Schools and educational practices are likely to be based more on philosophical beliefs rather than on empirical studies and theoretical understanding of learning. Schools are established according to regional, communal, and cultural beliefs about the world, the nature of humankind and children, the source of authority, and the subject of learning. Schools also differ in their beliefs about teaching and learning, but philosophical beliefs are often at the forefront. Every educational system and instructional program contains one or more theories of learning. Although these theories can be implicit, each has its unique importance to the functioning of the institution.

Some of the most important educational philosophers of Western civilization developed educational theories based on their practical experiences as tutors. As a result, much of their tutorial philosophies are developed into commonly used education principles today. Tutoring offers a powerful strategy to enhance student learning across a wide sampling of student needs and academic content areas. Furthermore, tutoring can allow students to develop higher level cognitive skills that enable them to understand and express complex ideas.

Educators should be concerned with theories and principles of human learning, teaching, and instruction. These need to be within the framework of theory-derived educational materials, programs, strategies, and techniques that enrich lifelong educational undertakings and approaches.

Three main categories or philosophical frameworks categorize learning theories: behaviorism, cognitivism, and constructivism. Behaviorism focuses on the objectively observable aspects of learning. Cognitive theories look further than behavior to explain brain-based learning. Cognitive learning encourages students to think for themselves, while brain-based learning takes a more interactive approach to learning. Constructivism views learning as a process in which the learner actively constructs or builds new ideas or concepts. The following section focuses on constructivism.

CONSTRUCTIVISM

Constructivism is a theory of knowledge with origins in philosophy, psychology, and cybernetics (Glasersfeld, 1989). In the 1930s and 1940s, constructivism was the prominent perspective among educators in American public schools. In the past decade, the constructivist learning theory has emerged as a prominent approach to teaching and learning. The word *constructivist* is an adjective derived from the noun *constructivism*. It specifies the theory about the nature of reality and the theory of knowledge.

The theory of constructivism looks at the way a learner learns. Constructivists believe that the learner learns best through active engagement. Constructivism therefore focuses on the importance of an individual's knowledge, beliefs, and skills through the experience of learning. Constructivism states that knowledge is created in individuals when information comes into contact with existing knowledge development by experiences. Individuals can accept new ideas and fit them into their established view of the world.

THEORETICAL BACKGROUND

Heather Kanuka and Terry Anderson (1998) suggest that constructivist learning theories began with the insights of Socrates, who claimed that the basic conditions for learning rest in the understanding of the individual. Nevertheless, John Dewey, an American philosopher, psychologist, and educational reformer, and Jean Piaget, a Swiss developmental philosopher and psychologist, are often cited as the founders of constructivism.

Other individuals who have provided historical precedents for the theory include Lev Vygotsky, a Russian philosopher and psychologist, and Jerome Bruner, an American psychologist. These individuals will be discussed later. Other influencers whose contributions have been significant to constructivism are Maria Montessori, an Italian physician and educator best known for her philosophy of education, and Ernst von Glasersfeld, an Austrian-born American philosopher and professor of psychology.

There are several forms of models in the literature of constructivism in education; however, two major forms are cognitive constructivism and social constructivism. These two constructivist views of learning are different in emphasis, though there is a great deal of overlap. The cognitive constructivism refers to how children develop cognitive abilities, and social constructivism suggests that reality takes on meaning that is formed and reformed through the social process.

John Dewey (1859–1952) rejected the notion that schools should focus on repetitive, rote memorization (Dewey, 1938). Dewey therefore proposed a method allowing students to engage in real-world, practical workshops where they could demonstrate their knowledge through creativity and collaboration. He believed that students should be provided with opportunities to think for themselves and articulate their thoughts.

Jean Piaget (1896–1980) is considered the chief theorist among cognitive constructivists. Piaget rejected the idea that learning was the passive assimilation of given knowledge. Instead, Piaget proposed that learning is a dynamic process comprised of successive stages of adaption to reality. During these stages, learners actively construct knowledge by creating and testing their own theories of the world. Piaget's theory of intellectual growth had a primary influence on the development of the current position of the constructivism.

Piaget (1970) advocates that children progress through the following sequence of four stages from birth to twelve years old:

1. Sensorimotor period—birth to two years
2. Preoperational thought—two to six or seven years
3. Concrete operations—six or seven years to eleven or twelve years
4. Formal operations—eleven or twelve years to adult

Piaget suggests that these stages predict what children can and cannot understand at specific ages. As a result, children cannot be taught key cognitive tasks if they have not reached a particular stage of development.

Piaget's theory of cognitive development suggests that humans cannot be given information and immediately understand and use it. Instead, learners must construct their own knowledge through experiences that enable them to create schemas (mental models of the world). Over time, these schemas are changed and enlarged and become more sophisticated through three complementary processes: assimilation, accommodation, and equilibration.

Assimilation occurs when a learner perceives new objects or events in terms of existing schemes or operations. Accommodation ensues when existing schemes or operations must be modified to account for a new experience. Equilibration is the master developmental process that encompasses both assimilation and accommodation. Differences of experience create a state of disequilibrium that can be resolved only when a more adaptive and sophisticated mode of thought is adopted.

Lev Vygotsky (1896–1934) is considered the major theorist among the social constructivists. Vygotsky's work was largely unknown to the West until it was published in 1962. Vygotsky shares many of Piaget's assumptions about how children learn, but Vygotsky places more prominence on the social context of learning. According to Vygotsky (1978), every function in the child's cultural development appears twice: first on the social level, and later on, on the individual level; first, between people (interpsychological) and then inside the child (intrapsychological). This applies equally to voluntary attention, to logical memory, and to formation of concepts. All the higher functions originate as actual relationships between individuals (p. 57).

Vygotsky believes that learning is fostered when children operate in the "zone of proximal development." The concept argues that with help from instructors and more advanced peers, learners can master concepts they cannot understand on their own. Vygotsky divided children's language development into three stages, at ages two, three, and seven. He said that at each stage, a child learns through observation and interaction with his or her direct social environment. The zone of proximal development model has the following two developmental levels:

1. The level of actual development—point the learner can reach and can problem-solve independently.
2. The level of potential development—point the learner is capable of attaining under the direction of educators or in collaboration with peers.

Drawing extensively on the work of Piaget (1952) and Vygotsky (1962), constructivist theorist Jerome Bruner (1990) emphasizes the role of the educator, language, and instruction. Bruner claims that learners use problem-solving processes that vary from person to person, a theory that puts social interaction at the core of good learning. Bruner is also considered a chief theorist among cognitive constructivists.

Bruner contends that learning is a social process, and therefore a process of discovery. Bruner initiated curriculum changes based on the notion that learning is an active process in which students construct new ideas or concepts based on their current knowledge.

Bruner provides the following principles of constructivist learning:

- Instruction must be concerned with the experiences and contexts that make the student willing and able to learn (readiness).
- Instruction must be structured so that students can easily understand it (spiral organization).
- Instruction should be designed to facilitate extrapolation and/or to fill in the gaps (going beyond the information given).

Methods of instruction or learning that apply constructivist learning theories and principles are derivative of conceptions as follows:

- Social activism—learning takes place in social environments where there are collaborative activities. These activities allow learners to communicate, interact, and learn from each other, consequently constructing their own world of knowledge.
- Scaffolding—the application of scaffolding (levels of cognitive functioning) refers to the process of learning in which guidance is provided from the basis of the student's experience. The process involves building on what students already know.
- Discovery learning—takes place in problem-solving situations where the learner draws on past experience and existing knowledge to discover facts, relationships, and new information. Students are therefore more likely to retain knowledge achieved by the engagement of real-world and contextualized problem solving.

RECOMMENDATIONS FOR TEACHING THE CONSTRUCTIVIST LEARNING THEORY

Jacqueline Brooks and Martin Brooks (1999) recommend the following educational strategies for teaching with the constructivist learning theory:

- Encourage and accept student autonomy and initiative.
- Include raw data and primary sources, manipulative, interactive, and physical materials.
- Use cognitive terminology, for example *classify*, *analyze*, *predict*, and *create*, when assigning tasks to students.
- Allow student responses to drive lessons, alter content, and change instructional strategies.
- Search out students' understanding and prior experiences about a concept before teaching it to them.
- Inspire students to engage in dialogue both with the educator and with each other.
- Encourage students' critical thinking and inquiry by probing them with thoughtful, open-ended questions, plus boost students to probe each other with questions.
- Ask follow-up questions and seek explanation after a student's initial response.
- Engage students in situations that might challenge their prior conceptions and create contradictions that encourage dialogue.
- After posing a question, allow students time to create relationships and answer thoughtfully by the construction of their own meaning.

The application of the constructivist approach to teaching enables tutors to make schoolwork much easier, even if it seemed complex before, because research reveals that tutoring empowers students' cognitive skills that enable them to understand and express complex ideas.

Certainly constructivism provides opportunities for independent thinking and allows students to take responsibility for their own learning by framing questions and analyzing them. In addition, constructivist learning allows students to establish connections between ideas and predict, justify, and support their ideas. Although there are differences between cognitive and social constructivism, they share common perspectives about teaching and learning.

The theories of learning and the constructivist learning theory offer stakeholders a deeper appreciation and understanding of theories. The theories are from educational experts that inform stakeholders. Stakeholders in return can use these theories to benefit students' learning within tutoring programs.

PURPOSE AND BENEFITS OF TUTORING PROGRAMS

Typically the purpose of tutoring is to prevent academic problems, provide remediation for students who encounter difficulties, maintain students' current academic status, or elevate students' academic abilities. Furthermore, tutoring allows students who encounter difficulties to reach a point at which they become successful independent learners.

All students benefit from at least one attentive individual who takes the time to discuss academic matters, personal problems, and the importance of performing well in school. Tutoring not only contributes to the acquisition of knowledge and skills for success, but also connects students with someone who cares. This connection can be a crucial factor that positively affects a student's experience at school. Such connectedness can lead to a higher level of student engagement, which is associated with higher attendance rates and test scores.

Tutoring provides the following benefits:

- Offers more individualized, structured, and systematic learning experiences.
- Improves academic achievement and personal growth.
- Encourages communication between student and tutor.
- Generates knowledge and understanding toward the specific subject matter and learning in general.
- Provides opportunities for questioning and clarification of difficult concepts.
- Offers additional review and practice of difficult material.
- Motivates self-paced and self-directed learning.
- Encourages higher levels of learning.
- Provides opportunity for intensive practice.
- Promotes self-esteem and self-confidence and improves study skills.
- Increases retention, persistence, and motivation to succeed.
- Reduces competition and provides praise, feedback, and encouragement.

Research suggests that tutoring programs need to have strong guidelines that guarantee unified instruction that helps tutors in their decision making. In addition, tutoring programs can benefit from the selection of one or several of the following tutoring formats.

TUTORING FORMATS

Tutoring formats that can be incorporated in a comprehensive tutoring program include one-on-one, home-based, peer, cross-age, small-group, online, volunteer, and after-school programs.

One-on-one tutoring has traditionally been one of the most effective forms of instruction, because the sessions can be personalized to fit each student's individual needs. One-on-one tutoring may take place in the general or special-education classroom, which makes it a viable alternative for generalized settings.

Home-based tutoring takes place within a student's home. More often than not, the tutor is also a parent, caregiver, sibling, or an individual hired by the student's family.

Peer tutoring is a form of tutoring based on cooperative learning, where students of the same or different abilities and/or age range work together. Generally in peer tutoring, higher achieving students are linked with lower achieving students or those with comparable achievement.

Cross-age tutoring is a peer tutoring approach that joins students of different ages, with older students assuming the role of tutor. Student pairing may include a variety of combinations, such as elementary students with high school students. In other cases, general-education students enrolled within an inclusive classroom are paired with children with special needs to help improve an academic skill.

Small-group tutoring takes place when a tutor leads a single session with a group of students who need assistance with the same material. The effectiveness of group tutoring is based on collaborative learning, where all members, guided by the tutor, are responsible for sharing their knowledge.

Online tutoring uses such tools as e-mail, computer conferencing, text messaging, whiteboard overlays, video, audio, and printed material for exchanging assignments and comments. Online tutoring is a resourceful way to reach a large number of students while maintaining individualized instruction and practice. Online tutoring can be as flexible as face-to-face instruction, though without the personal relationships between tutor and student.

Volunteer tutoring uses adults outside the school to tutor students. These adults include parents, community volunteers such as retirees, or undergraduate college students. Although volunteer tutors can never take the place of trained educators, they can provide tutoring, with supervision from trained educators, to obtain the guidance and skills needed to tutor effectively.

After-school programs that include tutoring are usually private or public nonprofit after-school institutions that work with philanthropies, the public, business sectors, and other nonprofit organizations to improve the effectiveness of programs and community initiatives, especially as they affect children.

Regardless of the format, tutoring helps solidify what students have learned or are struggling with in the classroom. Today increasing numbers of students are entering higher levels of education unprepared. Students who seek admission to colleges and universities sometimes seek tutoring for the Scholastic Aptitude Test or American College Test. In other cases, college juniors seek similar assistance to help them prepare for admission tests to medical college or law school. In addition, colleges and universities across the nation recognize the need to tutor students needing assistance in mastering a course.

Tutoring provides great benefits for students and must be planned and organized to be successfully implemented. Although no single program or intervention is effective for all students, tutoring presents opportunities to make a difference for our nation's students. Tutoring allows no child to be left behind and thus prepares them for the latest change—the Common Core State Standards.

POINTS TO REMEMBER

Tutoring has a long history as an effective and familiar strategy to strengthen classroom teaching and learning and to improve students' success in school, particularly because of the NCLB and its provisions for supplemental education services such as tutoring. Today it is essential to provide justification and documentation of the theoretical base that supports new instruction. As a condition of funding, many contemporary federal programs under the NCLB in kindergarten through grade twelve require that instructional practices and reform models be scientifically based. These programs include, for example, reading, supplementary educational services such as tutoring, and special education.

Learning theories are categorized under three main categories or philosophical frameworks: behaviorism, cognitivism, and constructivism. Behaviorism focuses on the objectively observable aspects of learning. Cognitive theories look further than behavior to explain brain-based learning. Cognitive learning encourages students to think for themselves, while brain-based learning takes a more interactive approach to learning. Constructivism views learning as a process in which the learner actively constructs or builds new ideas or concepts.

Typically tutoring prevents academic problems, provides remediation for students who encounter difficulties, maintains students' current academic status, or elevates students' academic abilities. Most important, tutoring allows even students who encounter difficulties to become successful independent learners.

All students benefit from at least one attentive individual who takes the time to discuss academic matters, personal problems, and the importance of performing well in school. A successful tutoring program hinges on the relationship between the tutor and the student. To establish a supportive relationship with their students, tutors must be open, respectful, and honest. Tutoring will ultimately benefit students by allowing them to face the world and others with openness and confidence.

Research has shown that one of the key reasons why tutoring has such a positive impact on student success is that it fosters social integration through the creation of a supportive relationship between tutor and student. Martha Bogart and Ruth Hirshberg (1993) state that tutors help improve retention rates, not only because they offer academic assistance, but also because they create relationships and bonds for students.

Tutoring programs can benefit from the selection of one or several tutoring formats, such as one-on-one, home-based, peer, cross-age, small-group, online, volunteer, and after-school programs that include tutoring. Tutors within these programs must endeavor not to take the place of skilled educators in their students' classrooms, but are to serve as supporters to help students learn.

Today, with our nation's increased attention focused on the achievements of students in school, it is important for individual tutors and/or tutoring establishments to show the value of what is being undertaken and the impact of their tutoring programs.

Chapter Two

Evaluation of Tutoring Programs

This chapter explains evaluation standards, types of evaluation, the program evaluation process, the importance and purposes of evaluation, and the role of evaluation in education. The chapter ends with a discussion of some common evaluation models and approaches that can be used in tutoring programs, including connoisseurship, objective-based, goal-free, adversary and judicial, Kirkpatrick's four-level, and Stufflebeam's CIPP.

THE IMPORTANCE AND PURPOSES OF EVALUATION

Evaluation is a relatively new field of knowledge and practice and has gained widespread attention during the late twentieth century (Stufflebeam & Coryn, 2013; Stufflebeam & Shinkfield, 2007). Since 1965, evaluations have grown considerably, because the United States government mandated that all educational programs that receive federal funding must spend a portion of those funds on program evaluation. The root of the term *evaluate* suggests that the function of evaluation is to place a value on the thing being assessed (Lincoln & Guba, 1980). Evaluation has been defined in many ways.

An evaluation is a purposeful, systematic, and careful collection and analysis of information. The information documents the effectiveness and impact of programs, establishes accountability, and identifies areas needing change and improvement. The term *program* is used as a general label for the various phenomena, such as individuals, institutions/organizations, methods, and materials that are the focus of educational evaluation. Evaluations may be conducted for programs of any size or scope.

In the public sector, formal evaluation was evident as early as 2000 BC, when Chinese officials conducted civil-service examinations to measure the proficiency of applicants for government positions. In education, Socrates used verbally mediated evaluations as part of the learning process (Fitzpatrick et al., 2010). In the 1800s evaluation of education and social programs began to take root in several countries. The beginnings of school accreditation for secondary schools and universities in the United States also originated during this era.

Scarvia Anderson and Samuel Ball (1978) describe the capabilities of program evaluation in terms of the following major purposes, which they believe are not mutually exclusive:

- To contribute to decisions about program installation, program continuation, expansion, certification, and program modifications
- To obtain evidence to gather support for a program or in opposition to a program
- To contribute to the understanding of basic psychological, social, and other processes

Michael Patton (2001) stated that the purpose of an evaluation is to make judgments about a program, improve its effectiveness, and/or inform programming decisions.

The first step in conducting an evaluation is therefore to determine its purpose. Most important is to determine if an evaluation is truly needed. If no funds are available, or if evaluative results cannot be used to make changes, perhaps the current time is not the best time for an evaluation.

The purposes of the evaluation are usually defined through consultation with the evaluator and the stakeholders. The stakeholders in a tutoring program might include tutors, teachers, or school administrators.

A program goal must be determined prior to the start of an evaluation. For example, in a tutoring program, the overall goal could be to determine student achievement in learning. It must be determined if the evaluation results will be used primarily for the improvement of the subject that is being imparted or if they are being used to identify the effectiveness of the program. The nature of the evaluation approach is likely to differ, depending upon which item has more importance.

Evaluation is essential to make certain decisions regarding the efficiency, effectiveness, or impact of a program. Efficiency refers to the degree to which a program or project has been productive in relationship to its resources. Effectiveness is about the degree to which goals have been reached. Impact denotes the degree to which a program or project resulted in changes. Overall, an evaluation looks at the results of an investment of time, expertise, and energy and compares the results with what must be achieved.

A program evaluation requires funding, time, and technical skills, and some people claim it often diverts program resources away from clients. Some program personnel are often concerned that evaluation activities deter timely accessibility to services. Research reveals that evaluation necessitates alliances among community groups such as academics, service providers, and advocacy groups (Short, Hennessy, & Campbell, 1996). Collaboration is therefore a key to successful program evaluation.

For decades, Robert E. Stake, a professor emeritus of education at the University of Illinois, Urbana-Champaign, has been a leader in the development of program evaluation methods. In 1967, Stake's writing on the "Countenance of Educational Evaluation" reoriented thinking about the nature of educational interventions and what items to pay attention to, to determine their effectiveness. Stake's writings and thinking in the field of program evaluation influenced the work of numerous scholars in the field.

In 2001, Stake identified that evaluation could be used as a tool to ensure quality, equality, and effectiveness in organizations that provide services to others. In addition, Stake believed that evaluation is for goodness and badness, merit and shortcoming, and quality. Two concepts that Stake affirms are central to evaluation are quality and representation.

Stake defines quality as the first and most important idea in evaluation and says that to evaluate is to recognize quality. On the other hand, Stake believes that in evaluation there is not only a need to discern quality, but also that representation conveys the sense of quality to others. Stake believes that evaluation should be widely known to stakeholders, and that it is irrational to provide clear evidence of quality if stakeholders misunderstand what is being evaluated.

Michael Scriven (1994) states that evaluation is the vital ingredient in every practical activity that distinguishes between the best thing and the less-good alternative, good practice and bad, good investigative designs and less-good ones, and good interpretations of theories and weaker ones. Ultimately, the purpose of an evaluation is to provide information to decision makers to enable them to make better decisions about programs, projects, or policies. Research indicates that evaluations are valuable and essential in any effective program.

THE ROLE OF EVALUATION IN EDUCATION

In the United States, evaluation—particularly program evaluation—had its beginning in the provisions of the Elementary and Secondary Education Act (ESEA). In 1965, President Lyndon B. Johnson signed the ESEA. It is an extensive statute that funds primary and secondary education, emphasizes equal access to education, and establishes high standards and accountability. As a result of the ESEA, the development of evaluation practices as a part of programs grew remarkably. The U.S. government mandated that all educational programs that received federal funding use a portion of the funds on program evaluation.

In 1966 as a result of national competition, the Center for the Study of Evaluation (CSE) was established and designated the first national center for research in educational evaluation. For more than forty years, the focus of the University of California Los Angeles (UCLA) CSE, and more recently the National Center for Research on Evaluation, Standards, and Student Testing (CRESST), has been the assessment of educational quality.

The CRESST is funded by the U.S. Department of Education's Office of Educational Research and Improvement and has been at the forefront of efforts to improve the quality of education and learning in America. The CRESST is a research partnership that consists of UCLA, the University of Colorado, Stanford University, RAND (Research and Development) Corporation, the University of Pittsburgh, the University of Southern California, Educational Testing Service, and the University of Cambridge in the United Kingdom.

The CRESST contributes to the development of scientifically based evaluation and testing techniques. It also encourages the development, validation, and use of sound data for improved accountability and decision making and explores technological applications to improve assessments and evaluations.

The National Center for Education Evaluation and Regional Assistance (NCEE) is one of the four centers of the Institute of Education Sciences (IES). The IES was established by the Education Sciences Reform Act of 2002 and brings rigorous and relevant research, evaluation, and statistics to America's education system.

The NCEE promotes the adoption of rigorous evaluation designs and methodologies in federal and nonfederal educational evaluation studies. Further, the NCEE supports synthesis and widespread distribution of results on rigorously conducted education research and evaluation. The results on effective programs and practices that advance student achievement are available to state and local educational agencies, institutions of higher education, Congress, parents, teachers, media, and the general public.

The NCEE supports the synthesis and widespread dissemination of results from evaluations and research through the work of the evaluation division and the knowledge utilization division. These programs include the following:

- The Regional Educational Laboratory Program—Designed to serve the educational needs of designated regions, it conveys the

latest, best research and proven practices into school improvement efforts.
- The What Works Clearinghouse (WWC)—Synthesizes the best evidence of the effectiveness of education programs, policies, and practices and reports on current research findings.
- The Education Resources Information Center (ERIC)—Provides access to the world's foremost databases of journal and nonjournal education literature.
- The National Library of Education—Collects and archives information, provides special historical and current collections of Department of Education documents, offers a collection of journals that supports the ERIC database and research reports that support the WWC, and delivers resources on current and historical federal education legislation.

The Center for Evaluation and Assessment (CEA) is located in the College of Education at the University of Iowa and has been in existence under charter since 1992. The CEA conducts a wide variety of program evaluations in collaboration with faculty across the University of Iowa campus and with school systems, colleges, and universities throughout Iowa and the United States.

Since the CEA was established it has completed fifty evaluations of educational and social programs. They include projects funded by the National Science Foundation, the National Institutes of Health (NIH), the United States Department of Education, the Iowa Department of Education, and the United States Department of Health and Human Services.

The Evaluation Center at Western Michigan University is committed to advancing theory, practice, and utilization of evaluation through research, education, service, and leadership. The center's principal activities are research, education, service, dissemination, and national and international leadership in evaluation.

The mission of the Evaluation Center is as follows:

- Provide evaluation, research, and capacity-building services to a broad array of university, public, community-based, national, and international organizations to assess and improve their programs.
- Conduct research on evaluation supported by federal grants to contribute to the evaluation knowledge base and advance theory and methodology of evaluation.
- Engage in academic leadership by publishing in peer-reviewed literature, by presenting on cutting-edge evaluation issues, and through service to professional organizations and scholarly journals.
- Administer the Interdisciplinary Doctor of Philosophy in Evaluation, which provides doctoral education and state-of-the-art research and evaluation opportunities for the next generation of evaluation scholars and practitioners.

During the late 1960s through the early 1980s, evaluations have proliferated; consequently, a significant number of educational researchers shifted into the field of evaluation research. The signing of the No Child Left Behind Act in 2002, which contained sweeping changes to the ESEA, also proposed the need for strong evaluation and accountability for programs and services. Specializing in evaluation are also social science journals such as the *Educational Review*, *Educational Evaluation and Policy Analysis*, and *Evaluation and Program Planning*. Besides, many school districts have established departments of evaluation. On the whole, educational evaluation has attracted considerable interest.

EVALUATION STANDARDS

Evaluation practices should adhere to the program evaluation standards developed by the Joint Committee on Standards for Educational Evaluation. As the importance of program evaluation increased, the Joint Committee was established in 1973 to develop a set of educational standards. The Joint Committee's Program Evaluation Standards suggest that "all evaluations will be conducted legally, ethically, and with due regard for the welfare of those involved in the evaluation as well as those affected by the results" (1994).

In 2014, the fourteen organizations that sponsor the Joint Committee on Standards for Educational Evaluation are as follow:

1. American Counseling Association
2. American Educational Research Association
3. American Evaluation Association
4. American Indian Higher Education Consortium
5. American Psychological Association
6. Canadian Evaluation Society
7. Canadian Society for the Study of Education
8. Consortium for Research on Educational Accountability and Teacher Evaluation
9. Council of Chief State School Officers
10. National Association of School Psychologists
11. National Council on Measurement in Education
12. National Education Association
13. National Rural Education Association
14. University Council for Educational Administration

The National Schools Boards Association is listed by the Joint Committee on Standards for Educational Evaluation as a cooperating organization.

To produce effective evaluations, the Joint Committee developed the following five categories of professional standards in 2011:

1. The utility standards are intended to ensure that an evaluation serves the information needs of intended users. Utility signifies an informative evaluation and is the degree to which an evaluation is instructive, timely, and helpful to individuals. The utility standards require that evaluation findings will serve the information needs of the intended users, primarily those implementing a project or those with some vested interest in it.

2. The feasibility standards are intended to ensure that an evaluation is effective and efficient. Feasibility is essentially the extent to which the evaluation design is cost effective and suitable to the setting in which the learning is to be directed. The feasibility standards direct evaluation to be cost effective, credible to the different groups who will use the evaluation information, and minimally disruptive to the project.

3. The propriety standards cover regulations, ethics, responsibilities, and tasks. They also focus on the evaluation practice in terms of legality, fairness, properness, and acceptability. The propriety standards are intended to ensure that an evaluation will be conducted legally, ethically, and with due regard for the welfare of those involved in the evaluation, as well as those affected by the results.

4. The accuracy standards are intended to ensure that an evaluation will reveal and convey technically adequate information about the features that determine worth or merit of the program being

evaluated. Accuracy refers to the outcome of the study and is the extent to which the evaluation produces valid, reliable, and thorough information for making judgments of the evaluated program's worth.

5. The evaluation accountability standards are intended to increase the use of adequate documentation and meta-evaluation. This encompassing attribute of evaluation quality results from balancing utility, feasibility, propriety, and accuracy. Internal and external meta-evaluation, discussed extensively in the accountability standards, provide the methodology used to increase and document evaluation quality.

Meta-evaluation is the process that examines and synthesizes several evaluation reports to judge the credibility and usefulness of the findings.

See appendix A for a more complete list of the Program Evaluation Standards Statements (Yarbrough et al., 2011) developed by the Joint Committee on Standards for Educational Evaluation.

TYPES OF EVALUATIONS

There are many types of evaluation, depending on the purpose, timing, and procedures used. Evaluations are generally divided into two broad categories: formative and summative.

A formative evaluation is also known as process, internal, or implementation evaluation. A formative evaluation conducted during program development and implementation examines aspects of an ongoing program to make changes or improvements as the program is being implemented. A formative evaluation can inform tutors of how well their instructional programs serve the objectives while the programs progress.

FORMATIVE AND SUMMATIVE EVALUATIONS

Wally Guyot (1978) stated that formative evaluation is useful in analyzing learning materials, student learning and achievements, and teacher effectiveness. A formative evaluation collects data and analyzes it at a time when program changes can be made, to ensure that the quality of the program implementation is sustained. For example, if a tutoring program has been introduced in a school district, it is significant to know to what extent the program has been implemented as designed. For formative evaluations, testing is important at all phases of tutoring—pretesting (before), embedded testing (during), and posttesting (after). Formative evaluation asks "How are we doing?"

The following are some examples of formative evaluation questions:

- Is the program being implemented as it was designed?
- Do the students or clients understand the program concepts?
- What are the misconceptions about the program?
- Are all program implementers implementing the program in the same way?
- Is the program being implemented on schedule?
- Is there sufficient time to implement all aspects of the program?
- What aspects of the program do not seem to be working as well as intended?
- Do the program implementers need additional training on the program?
- Are any negative outcomes developing?

A summative evaluation is also known as product, external, or outcome evaluation. A summative evaluation documents the results of a program and needs to be completed after a program is established. In a summative evaluation, specific goals of a program are identified and the degree of achievement of those goals is documented.

The results of a summative evaluation point to changes that need to be made in a program to improve it in subsequent implementations. In addition, summative evaluations can specify program status and conditions, for accountability purposes. The results can also be used as a needs assessment for the subsequent planning of changes in a program or for the introduction of new programs and interventions. Although pretesting, embedded testing, and posttesting are used in summative evaluations, posttesting is clearly the most critical and the main basis for forming conclusions about a tutoring program. Summative evaluation asks "How did we do?"

The following are some examples of summative evaluation questions:

- What did the program accomplish?
- Did the program reach its goals and objectives?
- What impact did the program have on its beneficiaries?
- What were the outcomes?
- Who benefited from the program?
- How much was the benefit?
- Was the benefit greater with the current program compared to another program?
- Did various types of students or clients benefit from the program?
- What were the positive outcomes?
- What were the negative outcomes?
- What should be improved/changed in the program?
- Does the benefit of the program warrant the cost?

PROGRAM EVALUATION PROCESS

Program evaluation involves the complete examination of a program, which includes its environment, client needs, procedures, and outcomes. The examination is accomplished by using a systematic data collection and analysis procedures. The program evaluation process suggested outlines the most important steps in planning, collecting data, and reporting results.

The suggested program evaluation process contains nine steps for planning, collecting data, and reporting results (Gooler, 1980; "Instructional Assessment Resources," 2011). These steps offer useful feedback to guide program development and improvement.

Step 1. Describe the program context

Descriptions convey the mission, goals, and objectives of the instructional program and include information about its purpose, expected effects, available resources, stage of development, and instructional context. Descriptions set the frame of reference for all subsequent planning decisions in an evaluation.

Step 2. Identify stakeholders and their needs

Stakeholders are the individuals and organizations involved in the program being evaluated or who might be affected by or interested in the findings of the evaluation. The identification of stakeholders at the beginning of an evaluation is vital. These individuals can explain the reason the evaluation was requested, formulate questions that should guide the evaluation, choose the design of the research, interpret results, and determine how the findings should be reported and to whom. Stakeholder needs generally reflect the central questions about the instructional program or activity. Determining stakeholder needs helps focus the evaluation process so that the results are of the greatest usefulness.

Step 3. Determine the evaluation purpose using central evaluation questions

Generally the purpose of an evaluation should be to establish the outcomes or worth of a program being provided and to find ways to improve the program. Three general purposes for instructional evaluations are as follows:

- Gain insight—Clarify how instructional activities should be designed to bring about expected changes
- Change practices—Improve the quality, effectiveness, or efficiency of instructional activities
- Measure effects—Examine the relationship between instructional activities and observed consequences

One of the most important questions is whether an evaluation is really needed. It is important to craft central evaluation questions clearly and completely. Evaluation questions can be stimulated by some sources that include program goals and objectives, strategic plans, mission statements, and national standards and guidelines.

Step 4. Identify intended uses

Intended uses are the specific ways evaluation results will be applied. They are the underlying goals of the evaluation and are linked to the central evaluation questions of the study that identify the specific aspects of the instructional program to be examined. The purpose, uses, and central questions of an evaluation are all closely related.

Step 5. Create an evaluation plan

The evaluation plan outlines how to implement the evaluation, including identification of the sponsor and resources available for implementing the plan, what information is to be gathered, the research method(s) to be used, a description of the roles and responsibilities of sponsors and evaluators, and a timeline for accomplishing tasks. A sponsor is the person or organization that hired or directed the evaluator to undertake a project. The sponsor is always a stakeholder.

Step 6. Collect data

Data collecting focuses on assembling information that conveys a complete picture of the instructional program and is seen as credible by stakeholders. Data collecting includes consideration about the following:

- Indicators—General concepts regarding the instruction, its context, and its expected effects into specific measures or variables that can be interpreted.
- Data sources and methods to use—Documents individuals and observations that provide information for the evaluation. Some potential data sources include students, parents, caregivers, school administrators, school board members, teachers, counselors, school psychologists, employers, documents, and other records.

Collection methods are the tools used to collect data. Some of the collection methods include the following:

- Document analysis—The systematic examination of program documents such as mission statements, training materials, and policy and procedures.
- Focus group—A group of similar individuals who provide information during a directed and moderated interactive group discussion.
- Interviews—A directed conversation with an individual using a list of questions designed to gather useful extended responses gathering in-depth information.
- Observation—The regular observation of program processes or operations using such things as checklists, scaled ratings, or narrative comments.
- Questionnaires and or surveys—A series of questions administered to individuals in a systematic manner.
- The data quality and data quantity—Data quality is the appropriateness and integrity of information collected and used in an evaluation. Data quantity is the amount of information collected for an evaluation.
- Human subject protections—A human subject is a living individual about whom the investigator obtains data through intervention or interaction with the individual or by identifiable private information.
- The context in which the data gathering occurs—Context sensitivity is being aware when doing research that the individuals and organizations under study have cultural preferences that dictate acceptable ways for asking questions and collecting information.

The amount of resources available for the program evaluation is a determining factor of how much data is collected. Interviewing all program partakers may be too expensive and time consuming, but a representative sample of the group might be ideal. A sample is a subset of the entire group information from which data is collected to draw conclusions about the entire group. The major goal in selecting the sample is to be sure that the group selected is representative of the entire population.

Several ethical issues arise during the collection and storing of data from human subjects when planning an evaluation. The American Evaluation Association developed *Guiding Principles for Evaluators* to promote ethical practice in the data-collecting process of program evaluation. A copy of the abbreviated version of *Guiding Principles for Evaluators* is available free by e-mail at the American Evaluation Association at office@eval.org or a copy in its entirety can be downloaded at http://www.eval.org/p/cm/ld/fid=51.

Data collected must also use multiple instruments that are valid (measure what they are supposed to measure) and reliable (produce similar results consistently).

Step 7. Analyze data

Data analysis involves identifying patterns in the data. This goal is accomplished by isolating important findings or by combining sources of information to reach a larger understanding and making decisions about how to organize, classify, interrelate, compare, and display information. These decisions are guided by questions being asked, the types of data available, and the input from stakeholders.

The data collected is analyzed and presented in the form of tables and graphs. Statistical tools are often used to compare significant differences and establish correlation or relationship between variables. In many cases, introductory-level knowledge of statistics will be sufficient for completing the data analysis; nevertheless, more complex analysis may require assistance from a statistical consultant.

Four typical analysis procedures are frequency distributions; frequency graphs or histograms; descriptive statistics, such as percentages, means, and medians; and a listing of actual comments made by respondents. The first three are quantitative analyses, and the fourth is qualitative.

Quantitative analyses gather numerical data that can be summarized through statistical procedures. Conversely, qualitative analysis collects nonnumerical data, usually textual, that can also provide rich details about a program. A good evaluation usually combines both types of analyses. Each approach has its particular strengths, and when used together, they offer a comprehensive representation of a program.

Step 8. Conclusions and recommendations

Conclusions are linked to the evidence collected and judged against agreed-upon standards set by stakeholders. Recommendations are actions for consideration that are based on conclusions, but go beyond simple judgments about efficacy or interpretation of the evidence collected.

Step 9. Reporting

Factors to consider when reporting results, or dissemination, include tailoring report content for a specific audience, explaining the focus of the study and its limitations, and listing both the strengths and weaknesses of the study. It may also include the reporting of active follow-up and interim findings. Tutors or staffs sometimes use interim findings to make immediate instructional adjustments. Some stakeholders can receive a comprehensive and detailed report, while in other cases, a short executive summary will suffice. The information must be personalized to the needs and wants of the particular stakeholder.

Generally an evaluation designed by a tutoring program should adhere to the guidelines found in the Joint Committee on Standards for Educational Evaluation (2011). See appendix A.

EVALUATION MODELS AND APPROACHES

The evaluation model most appropriate for a particular program is determined after clarifying the purpose of an evaluation and the targeted audience for the results. The conduct of a program evaluation, therefore, involves the selection of an appropriate evaluation model or approach.

Today there are several models and approaches from which to select, so the selection of a suitable evaluation model requires thoughtful consideration. Between 1986 and 1996, nearly sixty evaluation models were developed, and in one meta-evaluation, twenty-two models were compared.

Barbara Flagg indicated that the connoisseur-based, objectives-based, and decision-oriented models are classified as commonly used evaluation models (1990; 2013). The following section highlights the above models and others regularly mentioned in evaluation literature.

CONNOISSEURSHIP

The term *connoisseurship* was devised in the 1980s by Elliot Eisner, an art educator. Eisner is particularly known for his work in arts education, curriculum studies, and educational evaluation. He defined connoisseurship as the art of appreciation that can be displayed in any realm in which the character, import, or value of objects, situations, and performances is distributed and variable, including educational practice (Eisner, 1998).

The word *connoisseurship* comes from the Latin *cognoscere*, meaning to know (Eisner, 1998). It involves the ability to see, not only to look. Eisner has applied the concepts of connoisseurship and criticism, terms familiar in the world of arts, to the study of educational practice (1998).

The connoisseurship evaluation model is grounded in the professional expertise of the program evaluators as they evaluate a program, organization, product, or activity (Eisner, 1976). The connoisseurship evaluation model uses the concept of the connoisseur as an evaluator who enters an organization and serves as a critic of the program under review. Eisner (2002) indicates that this approach entails two positions: connoisseurship and criticism.

The first position, connoisseurship, is the method that appreciates the qualities of an educational program and its significance. To perform the role well, the connoisseur must have professional knowledge of the program being evaluated as well as of other related programs. The next position, criticism, is the art that reveals the qualities of events or objects that connoisseurship identifies. It is the method that explains and assesses the process that describes and evaluates what has been recognized.

Connoisseurs or evaluators may be expected to consider guidelines and criteria, but the standards they use to reach their judgments are primarily derived from their collective experience of the profession. The quality of educational connoisseurship and criticism therefore relies extensively on the expertise of the evaluator. The evaluator transforms the instrument, and the data collecting, analyzing, and judging are generally concealed within the evaluator's mind. The training, experience, and credentials of the evaluator are critical, because the validity of an evaluation depends on the evaluator's opinion.

OBJECTIVE-BASED

Objective-based evaluation models have the contribution of numerous individuals. Ralph Tyler (1950) is recognized for the conceptualization and dissemination of objectives-based evaluation in education. In the 1940s, Tyler's work on curriculum evaluation brought about a major change in educational evaluation. He believed that curricula offered should be grouped around specific goals, and success should be based on how students are able to achieve the goals successfully.

The purpose of the objective-based evaluation model is to move from the evaluation of individual students to the evaluation of the curriculum. As a result, the model allows the evaluator to identify if a student's achievement might be poor because of a lack of natural ability, rather than a weakness in the curriculum.

Evaluation in this model involves the process that determines the extent to which the objectives of a program were actually attained (Tyler, 1950). Tyler's approach to evaluation uses the following steps:

1. Establishment of broad goals or objectives
2. Classification of the goals or objectives
3. Definition of objectives in behavioral terms
4. Discovery of situations in which achievement of objectives can be revealed
5. Development or selection of measurement techniques
6. Collection of performance data

7. Comparison of performance data with behaviorally stated objectives. Any difference between stated objectives and achievement of those objectives would cause revisions or modifications to correct such deficiencies.

Tyler's model has contributed to a significant influence on continuous developments in educational evaluation. In the 1960s, the National Assessment of Educational Progress (NAEP), a federal program that maintained data on the academic achievement of the youth of America, emerged under Tyler's leadership. Another outgrowth of the Tyler model has been the increased practice of competency testing of students and teachers. Tyler's principles are logical, scientifically acceptable, and readily followed by evaluators. His principles were very influential on later evaluation theorists (Fitzpatrick et al., 2010).

GOAL-FREE

The goal-free evaluation model was developed by Michael Scriven in 1973. Goal-free evaluation rests on the foundation that an evaluation should examine the value of a program by examining what it is undertaking, instead of what it is attempting to accomplish. Goal-free therefore focuses on the actual outcomes, rather than the intended outcomes of a program. In this evaluation, the evaluator is unaware of the stated or implied goals and objectives of the program.

The principle of goal-free evaluation is that the goals should not be taken as a given and should be evaluated. Scriven (1994) was convinced that the most significant purposes of goal-free evaluation were to decrease bias and increase objectivity. The following represented major features of goal-free evaluation (Fitzpatrick et al., 2010):

1. The evaluator deliberately avoids becoming aware of the program goals.
2. Predetermined goals are not allowed to limit the focus of the evaluation study.
3. Goal-free evaluation focuses on definite outcomes, rather than intended program outcomes.
4. The goal-free evaluator has minimal contact with the program manager and staff.
5. Goal-free evaluation increases the likelihood that unanticipated side effects will be noted.

Goal-free evaluation has merit, but there are many circumstances under which an evaluator is expected to collect evaluative data about specific program goals. In these situations, however, the evaluator can still address the stated goals and remain alert to the possibility that the program may have actual consequences that can be both advantageous and detrimental and can be unlike the consequences intended by the program developers.

ADVERSARY AND JUDICIAL

Tom Owens (1973) and Robert Wolf (1975) independently developed evaluation approaches that are typically categorized as adversary evaluation models. Judicial or adversary evaluations are grounded on judicial representation.

Adversary evaluation uses an argumentative approach and is modeled on procedures that originate from the field of law. It is distinguished by the use of a wide collection of data and the hearing of evidence, meaning that opposing sides present positive and negative judgments about the program being evaluated.

The following are four stages for an adversary evaluation (Crabbé & Leroy, 2008; Gall et al., 2007; and Thurston, 1978):

1. The issue generation stage—Produces a wide range of issues regarding the program by examining various stakeholders.
2. The issue selection stage—Restricts the issues to a manageable number.
3. The preparation of arguments stage—Collects data, locates relevant documents, and synthesizes available information as it pertains to the program.
4. The hearing stage—Conducts prehearing sessions and official hearings in which the adversarial team presents its position before those who must make a decision about the program. This stage is followed by the presentation of evidence and a panel deliberation and recommendations.

Adversary evaluation has proved useful to reveal the strengths and weaknesses of programs, and it creates questions that require explanations. An adversary evaluation, however, requires a great deal of time and a considerable number of individuals; consequently, it is costly, and few adversary evaluations are found in the educational research literature (Gall et al., 2007). Fitzpatrick et al. (2010) saw the common strategy of adversary hearings as a creative and effective way to present information to any size audience and get the audience to judge the merits of the arguments.

The judicial evaluation approach, as adversary approach, is also modeled on procedures that originate from the field of law. The approach is an adaptation of legal procedures for an evaluative framework. Unlike legal adversary hearings, the objective of this approach is not to win, but to provide comprehensive understanding of a program.

The judicial model simulates the use of legal procedures to promote a broad understanding of a program. In addition, it simplifies the understated and presents recommendations and policy guidelines that result in institutional development and an improved practice. The model assumes that it is impossible for an evaluator not to have a personal impact. The model therefore aims at teaching the involved stakeholders and the attending public about the program.

As mentioned in adversary evaluation, the following are the four stages of judicial evaluation (Crabbé & Leroy, 2008; Gall et al., 2007; and Thurston, 1978):

1. The issue generation stage
2. The issue selection stage
3. The preparation of arguments stage
4. The hearing stage

According to Gall et al. (2007), the judicial evaluation model, unlike adversary evaluation, does not involve a debate between two evaluation groups with conquest or persuasion as the desired outcome. Nonetheless, supporters of the judicial model stress the importance of carefully adapting the model to the setting in which it is used and toward the program it aims to address. Research indicates that judicial evaluations have proved useful in both formative and summative evaluations of educational programs.

KIRKPATRICK'S FOUR-LEVEL

Donald Kirkpatrick's four-level evaluation model is the most commonly used learning and training evaluation approach. In 1959,

Donald Kirkpatrick defined the model in a series of articles that appeared in the *Journal of the American Society of Training Directors*, now known as *Training and Development Magazine*.

Kirkpatrick's model has the following four levels of evaluation:

- Level 1: Reaction—Evaluates the feelings and reactions of learners on education teaching. It covers satisfaction of learners on teaching arrangement, courses, teachers (tutors), teaching materials, and teaching methods.
- Level 2: Learning—Aims at understanding learners' comprehension of instruction, principles, ideas, knowledge and skills.
- Level 3: Behavior—Assesses learners' changes of behaviors after teaching, to measure how learners apply what is learned in actual work.
- Level 4: Results—Focuses on influence of learners' behavior on teaching results.

In Kirkpatrick's four-level model, evaluation should begin with level one, and if the organization's time and budget allows, the evaluation moves sequentially through levels two, three, and four. The evaluation becomes more complex, expensive, important, and meaningful as it progresses from level 1 to level 4. In some organizations it may not be desirable, practical, or necessary to perform all levels in the model. Each successive level, however, represents a more accurate measure of the effectiveness of a program and requires more time-consuming analysis at increased costs.

In Kirkpatrick's four-level model, each prior level functions as a foundation for the next level. Each organization needs to select the level that will produce the information required to evaluate its particular program. According to Kirkpatrick and Kirkpatrick (2006), it is extremely critical that professionals evaluate learning programs for three main reasons, to justify the existence and budget of the organization by showing how it contributes to the organizational objectives and goals, to decide to continue or discontinue programs, and to gain information on how to improve future programs.

THE STUFFLEBEAM CIPP

The Stufflebeam CIPP evaluation was developed by Daniel Stufflebeam and colleagues in the late 1960s. They developed a model to improve and achieve accountability for U.S. school projects, in particular, projects geared toward improvement of teaching and learning in urban school districts. Over the years, the Stufflebeam CIPP has been further developed and used in many other countries, as well as inside and outside of educational settings.

Stufflebeam's model defines evaluation as the process to delineate, obtain, and provide useful information for judging decision alternatives. The definition contains three important points. First, evaluation is a systematic, continual process. Second, the evaluation process includes three basic steps: (a) it delineates questions to be answered and information to be obtained, (b) it obtains relevant information, and (c) it provides information to decision makers who can consequently improve ongoing programs. Third, evaluation serves the decision-making process.

Stufflebeam's CIPP evaluation model is a comprehensive framework to conduct evaluations of programs, projects, personnel, products, organizations, and evaluation systems. The acronym CIPP, by which the model is well known, stands for evaluations of an entity's context, input, process, and product.

1. Context evaluation assesses needs, problems, assets, and opportunities to pinpoint objectives. It includes the examination and

describes the context of the program being evaluated. Context evaluation helps in making program-planning decisions.

2. Input evaluation considers alternative approaches; for example, a comparison of how a program might perform compared to other programs, staffing plans, and budgets for their feasibility and potential cost-effectiveness to meet targeted needs and achieve goals. Input evaluation examines what a program will be doing and aids in making program structuring decisions.

3. Process evaluation includes the examination of how a program is being implemented, monitors how the program is performing, reviews the program to ensure it is following required legal and ethical guidelines, and identifies defects in the procedural design or in the implementation of the program. In general, process evaluation helps in making implementation decisions.

4. Product evaluation provides information that determines whether objectives are being achieved and whether the procedure employed to achieve them should be continued, modified, or terminated. Product evaluation is very helpful in making summative evaluation decisions; for example, what is the merit and worth of the program? Should the program be continued?

In 2005, Gullickson revealed that the Stufflebeam CIPP evaluation model was consistent with a wide variety of program evaluations and was used to advance theory, practice, and use of educational evaluations. The CIPP evaluation model is recommended for individual educators, groups of educators, schools, systems of schools, and similar groups in disciplines outside education.

There is a wide selection of evaluation models and approaches. Some additional evaluation models and approaches mentioned in evaluation literature are the behavioral-objectives approach, consumer-oriented approaches, empowerment evaluations, expertise/accreditation approaches, organizational learning, participatory/collaborative evaluations, responsive evaluations, theory-driven evaluations, utilization-focused evaluations, and the success-case method. Each model and approach offers evaluators a foundation to evaluate a program, product, process, or activity.

A program evaluation that focuses on quantitative student achievement data and an array of qualitative data gives stakeholders meaningful information to make informed decisions regarding instructional programming, the delivery of support and services, and the impact of a program, such as tutoring programs, on expected student outcomes.

POINTS TO REMEMBER

For centuries evaluations have been useful tools that determine improvement toward or accomplishments of the objectives specified by any program. Program evaluation serves as a valuable tool in a tutoring program and helps stakeholders focus resources on the elements of a program most beneficial to the students and tutors. An evaluation's main purpose is to provide information for decision making and to improve the quality of a program by identifying program strengths and weaknesses. The findings allow organizations to promote learning and improve organizational effectiveness.

Evaluations should be a continuous process. Research reveals that regular and systematic program evaluation is one of the most effective practices related to significant student achievements (Moss et. al., 2001). A poorly designed evaluation program can hinder student advancement, though, so adherence to best practices is vital to guarantee that students achieve better success. Sufficient funds must therefore be allocated to support evaluation functions.

To be useful and worthwhile, an evaluation does not have to be complex, highly statistical, or in need of specialized experts. Sometimes the best evaluations are conducted by people who know and care about the program and its effects on students. Based on an individual's or an organization's budget and the complexity of the design plan, an individual or members of a design team can conduct a program evaluation. These internal evaluators, as they are sometimes called, are usually experts in the program and can directly benefit by collecting evaluation data firsthand. Outside experts or external evaluators may be used, but they add cost to a program. External evaluators do, however, deliver expertise and improve credibility and objectivity because they are not personally involved in a program's success.

An excellent resource that helps evaluators and practitioners choose a suitable evaluation method is the Harvard Family Research Project (http://www.hfrp.org/evaluation). The project was developed by the Harvard Graduate School of Education in Cambridge, Massachusetts. The project's evaluation tools can be used for first-time internal evaluations or large-scale national studies.

The Harvard Family Research Project was developed in 1983 and has a strategic leadership and research impact. The project strives to increase the effectiveness of public and private organizations and communities as they promote such things as student achievement and learning. The project focuses national attention on the idea that a systemic approach that integrates school and nonschool supports better ensures that all children have the skills they need to succeed.

In 2007, Wilder Research identified the following programs that have evaluation results: Book Buddies, Books and Beyond, Early Identification Program, Helping One Student to Succeed, Howard

Street Tutoring Program, ICARE, Intergenerational Tutoring Program, Juel's (1996) program, Prevention of Learning Disabilities, School Volunteer Development Project, Success for All, TEACH (Teacher Education Assistance for College and Higher Education), Wallach and Wallach Tutorial Program, and Wallach Tutoring Program.

A well-designed, thoughtful, and carefully implemented evaluation offers important information to document the results of a program such as tutoring programs and points stakeholders to areas where improvements may be needed. According to Weiss (1972) and Weissbord (1973), evaluation provides the evidence on which to base decisions about the maintenance, institutionalization, and expansion of successful programs and the modification or abandonment of unsuccessful ones. Tutoring is, however, most useful when certain components of successful tutoring programs are observed. These components are discussed in chapter 3.

Chapter Three

Successful Tutoring Programs

This chapter discusses tutoring and interpersonal relationships and the effective components of successful tutoring programs. It provides a list of the core essentials for tutors in successful tutoring programs too. The chapter ends with highlighting the Reading Recovery tutoring program and three best practices for after-school tutoring programs.

TUTORING AND INTERPERSONAL RELATIONSHIPS

Martha Adler (1999) and Susan Gibbs (2014) state that successful tutoring programs are those that screen, train, and monitor tutors; judiciously match students and tutors; and preserve close relationships. Successful tutoring programs also convene key stakeholders who contribute to and benefit from the program. Stakeholders include students, tutors, tutor recruiters and coordinators, administrators, reading specialists, educators, parents, caregivers, and staff from community organizations.

Tutors in successful tutoring programs build strong interpersonal relationships with their students, so tutors must be open, respectful, and honest. The more connected students feel to their tutors, the more trust and respect are formed, and these elements are central to student success. Several researchers have recognized that tutor effectiveness is essentially based on tutors' ability to provide both an interpersonal connection and academic support (Tinto, 1997; Bogart & Hirshberg, 1993; Pascarella et al., 1986; Pascarella & Terenzini, 1983).

A research conducted on cross-age tutoring programs revealed that the most successful tutoring programs put emphasis on training tutors in interpersonal, management, and content skills (Marious, 2000). Most important is that these skills should be planned in advance (Rekrut, 1994). Interpersonal skills include the ability to provide assistance and offer encouragement and positive feedback to students. Management skills deal with creating a proper work environment, using proper lesson materials, and establishing helpful seating arrangements and a setting conducive to learning. Content skills involve planning activities, follow-up activities, and questioning procedures.

A tutor's role is unique and involves exhibiting the friendliness of a friend, inspiration of a mentor, strength of an authority figure, and knowledge of an instructor (Schmidt, 2011). Schmidt further stated that a tutor has a distinct role that is defined by formal guidelines and the patterns of communication in which they engage. Understanding the way in which tutors and students engage in interpersonal communication patterns allows for better understanding and the definition of the unique role. Once the unique role is better understood, Schmidt states, tutors can develop critical communication skills to build connections that increase student success.

The perspective on communication started in the early twentieth century with Cooley's (1902) claim that relationship is necessary for a sense of self. Cooley's idea of the *looking-glass self* describes how individuals perceive themselves according to the way they assume others perceive them. An interpersonal perspective on communication suggests that the reciprocal nature of communication between individuals shapes one's sense of self and leads to the identification of unique roles.

With individualized attention tailored to the specific needs of the student being tutored, tutors are in exceptional position to advance their students' learning. Interpersonal relationships in a tutoring program need to be established around appropriate settings that are open, quiet, convenient, and away from distractions. They must also have good lighting, comfortable seating, a table for writing activities, and a place to store materials.

Throughout tutoring, other individuals are integral parts of students' lives and will also influence them in many ways. These people may include parents, caregivers, teachers, and administrators of students' school or tutoring facilities. Although recognizable differences and commonalities between tutors and students might exist, such as cultural, ethnic, or socioeconomic backgrounds, successful tutoring relationships can still be created.

EFFECTIVE COMPONENTS OF SUCCESSFUL TUTORING PROGRAMS

Researchers who have examined multiple tutoring programs have stressed a number of specific components that increase the quality of tutoring programs. The following discusses the effective components of successful tutoring programs that improve the chances for a positive impact on student achievement.

INTENSITY, CONSISTENCY, AND STRUCTURE

Tutoring programs need to be intensive, consistent, and structured. As for structure, Brailsford (1991) indicates that tutoring programs offering instruction from ten to sixty minutes in length resulted in positive outcomes for students. Brailsford noted that longer sessions did not necessarily lead to higher student achievements.

The U.S. Department of Education (1997) and Reisner et al. (1990) stated that tutoring programs in which tutors meet with students at least three times a week were more likely to generate positive achievement for students than programs in which tutors and students meet twice a week. Most important, researchers indicate that while the number of weekly sessions can vary between two and four a week, ten to sixty minutes in length ensures that students benefit from tutoring and there is a preservation of close relationships between the tutor and student. Overall, more sessions a week result in greater improvements. Tutoring is, however, most effective when tutors and students are dedicated and faithful in attendance.

Consistency over an extended period of time is also important in tutoring programs. The more time students have to work on a skill, the more opportunity they have to master that skill. In a 2011 study conducted by Nelson-Royes and Reglin, it was revealed that better tutoring results occurred for every student whose attendance to the tutoring programs was consistent.

A 1982 meta-analysis conducted by Cohen et al. found that structured tutoring programs demonstrated higher achievement gains than unstructured programs. In 1997, the U.S. Department of Education indicated that well-structured tutoring programs in which the content and delivery of instruction is thoughtfully scripted revealed higher achievement gains than unstructured programs.

USING A DIAGNOSTIC/DEVELOPMENTAL TUTORING PROGRAM

When individual diagnosis is structured into a tutoring program, long-term student achievement increases. According to Gordon et al. (2004; 2007) and Gordon (2009) a diagnostic/developmental template should be used to organize the tutoring program for each student. An effective method of individual diagnosis has tutors observe and record student learning skills on a session-by-session basis (Vellutino et al., 1996). This method allows a more accurate diagnosis of specific learning obstacles.

The diagnostic/developmental approach in tutoring programs helps tutors discover subtle underlying cognitive-processing issues such as dyslexia, visual/auditory perceptual issues, and attention-span limitations (Gordon et al., 2004).

INTENSIVE AND ONGOING TRAINING AND FEEDBACK FOR TUTORS

Well-trained tutors are critical to a successful tutoring program. Highly trained tutors consistently produce better tutoring outcomes. Mathes and Fuchs (1994) and Shanahan and Barr (1995) state that a tutor's professional education, degrees, special credentials, prior professional experience, and specialized training contribute to ensure that students achieve better long-term learning improvements. Wasik and Slavin (1993) and Moss et al. (2001) recognized that tutoring programs that produce the most impact are those in which tutors received more extensive training.

Research, however, reveals that even tutors with minimal training can have a positive impact on students' academic achievement, especially if the tutors are carefully supervised by an experienced educator. Tutors with minimal training should have regular supervision, however, as well as ongoing training and feedback during the course of tutoring.

The Kingsbury Center is an example of an institution that has continual tutor training. Since 1938, the Kingsbury Center has been a leading independent educational institution that provides tutoring services to children and adults throughout the District of Columbia, Maryland, and Virginia. The center's certified tutors receive special training, as well as ongoing professional development to keep their skills current. Prospective tutors must have a bachelor's degree, preferably in education or a related field, and have some teaching experience.

Tutors are most effective when they receive comprehensive training and ongoing support. Individuals of various ages and levels of education can be effective tutors, once provided appropriate training.

SYSTEMATIC REFLECTIVE ASSESSMENT OF STUDENT PROGRESS BY TUTORS

Reflection on the part of the tutor is a means that improves the quality of tutoring instruction. Roskos et al. (2001) states that rather than being based on opinions, reflection goes to the heart of the instructional relationship, and it is not only a tool of skilled practice, but also a feeling that helps educators teach effectively and intelligently.

Research on effective components of tutoring programs advocates well-structured, systematic programs that are assessment-based (Invernizzi & Ouellette, 2001; Topping, 1998). According to Roe and Vukelich (2001), the assessment of a tutoring program has to be ongoing, with adequate feedback given to tutors and students. Tutoring sessions need to be assessed continually to ensure their day-to-day integrity.

CLOSE COORDINATION WITH TEACHER AND CLASSROOM

Whether a student is tutored in or out of school, collaboration with the student's classroom teacher is vital to a tutoring program's success or failure (Gordon, 2009; and Gordon et al., 2004). The interchange between the subject area teacher and the student's tutor provides a mutual benefit and enhances tutoring sessions. The tutor helps improve instruction for the student in the regular classroom, and the regular classroom teacher conveys important information to the tutor. As the tutoring partnership progresses, the student realizes a clearer link between tutoring and classroom work. Students' association to their school setting is central to their academic improvement.

In 2009 a research conducted by the Center for Prevention Research and Development also found that the best performing tutoring programs have the following qualities: trained tutors, especially novice tutors, on effective instructional strategies; a diagnostic/developmental outline; formal and informal assessment for each student; tracking by tutors of students' progress; collaboration with students' classroom teachers; and structuring of tutoring programs around principles of learning.

CORE ESSENTIALS FOR TUTORS IN SUCCESSFUL TUTORING PROGRAMS

- Treat students with respect
- Remember that errors provide the best opportunities for teaching and learning
- Be patient
- Recognize individual differences and commonalities—important for building a tutoring relationship
- Be supportive of students' efforts as well as of their accomplishments
- Be positive
- Make tutoring sessions lively
- Do not use bribes or rewards to motivate students
- Be on time and committed
- Be open-minded
- Incorporate students' interests into activities and assignments
- Be creative
- Be flexible
- Set educated goals and strive for them
- Be trustworthy
- Be attentive
- Be precise by providing clear and direct instructions
- Establish priorities
- Be diligent and work from the beginning to the end of the tutoring session
- Offer praise
- Be results oriented

NATIONAL TUTORING ASSOCIATION (NTA) TUTOR CODE OF ETHICS

The NTA, founded in 1992, is the oldest and largest professional association devoted to supporting student success through tutoring. The association includes individuals who are interested in tutoring, such as peer tutors, paraprofessional tutors, professional tutors, literacy volunteers, tutor trainers and administrators, and private tutors. The NTA represents the interest of thousands of tutors in the United States and other countries. The NTA members represent elementary, middle, and high schools; colleges; universities; school districts; literacy programs; community programs; grant-supported programs; and No Child Left Behind/Supplemental Educational Services providers.

The NTA Tutor Code of Ethics provides members with opportunities to achieve and maintain high professional standards for tutors and administrators of tutoring programs and services. The following are the NTA Tutor Code of Ethics (2013):

- I understand that my role as a tutor is to enable students to do their own work using the best learning approach possible.
- I will provide honest feedback in the form of positive praise and/or constructive suggestions to the student I serve in a manner that will be beneficial to their overall learning.
- I will demonstrate faith in my student's learning abilities.
- I understand that my relationship to the student is professional and not personal.
- I will show respect for my student's cultural background and personal value system.
- I recognize that I may not have all the answers to student questions. In this event, I will seek assistance in finding answers to

the student's questions and/or direct the student to an appropriate resource for the information.
- I will maintain accurate records of tutoring sessions as expected and required.
- I will respect my student's personal dignity at all times.
- I will be on time for tutoring appointments, not only out of courtesy, but also to set a good example for my student to follow.
- I will keep information confidential about the student I am assigned.
- I understand that my ultimate goal is to assist my student in discovering how he or she best learns and to help my student develop the skills to achieve his or her best educational outcome.
- I will share any concerns I have with my supervisor.
- I expect to learn along with my student.
- I will keep current in both my subject area(s) and learning methodologies.
- I will remain flexible to my approach to student learning, respectful to the various learning styles and preferences.
- I will share techniques for improved study skills with my students.

Overall, a successful tutoring partnership fosters a mutual trust between the tutor and student; though throughout tutoring, other stakeholders, such as parents, educators, and administrators become an integral part of the tutoring connection.

READING RECOVERY TUTORING PROGRAM

Tutoring has been greatly influenced by tutoring programs such as the Reading Recovery (RR), which also contains components essential in successful tutoring programs. The RR is a successful, typically in-school tutoring program used in about 6,000 schools (United Way Worldwide, 2011). The RR was developed in the 1970s by educator Dr. Marie Clay at the University of Auckland in New Zealand.

According to the What Works Clearinghouse (2008), the RR is a time-tested program that has moderate to large positive effects on students' general reading achievement and is the highest rated program of its kind. The What Works Clearinghouse is a government agency that independently evaluates reports on educational programs and interventions.

The RR is one of the most influential tutoring programs for early learners who have failed after a year to adequately respond to formal reading instruction. In this program, first-grade students who struggle in reading and writing receive short-term one-on-one tutoring. The program promotes literacy skills and fosters development of reading and writing strategies. This development is tailored by one-on-one tutoring lessons that accommodate individual student needs. Tutoring is delivered by trained teachers in daily thirty-minute pull-out sessions over the course of twelve to twenty weeks. Teacher training includes a one-year university-based training program and ongoing professional development.

The RR has been widely researched throughout the world. Educators reveal that the RR is among the best evidence of the direct link between a good design and education excellence. Other well-researched tutoring programs that contain components of successful tutoring programs include Success For All (SFA), Howard Street Tutoring Program, and Book Buddies. The RR, SFA, and the Howard Street Tutoring Programs have been rigorously evaluated in comparison to control groups.

BEST-PRACTICE TUTORING PROGRAMS

The Saint Paul Public Schools (SPPS) Foundation, 826 National, and Building Educated Leaders for Life (BELL) are examples of organizations that strive to institute best-practice tutoring programs. These programs incorporate several of the effective components of successful tutoring programs previously discussed. The following are highlights of the SPPS Foundation, 826 National, and BELL tutoring programs:

SPPS FOUNDATION

The SPPS Foundation is an independent nonprofit organization that exists to mobilize resources to support student success in Saint Paul Schools, a school district that serves the city of Saint Paul in Minnesota. It is the state's largest school district and serves more than 38,000 students and employs more than 5,300 teachers and staff members. The SPPS Foundation serves a bridge between the school district and the community. It also makes grants to teachers, schools, and community organizations and coordinates programs such as the Tutoring Partnership.

Since 2007, the SPPS Foundation has convened the Tutoring Partnership for Academic Excellence (Tutoring Partnership) at the request of and in collaboration with SPPS. The Tutoring Partnership is a learning community where tutoring programs share and scale effective practices. By coordinating this learning community within a collective impact framework, the SPPS Foundation efficiently leverages resources that improve program quality and student outcomes.

The Tutoring Partnership did the following to achieve its goals in 2013–2014:

- Organized eighteen community organizations that serve 6,721 students with 1,696 tutors around a common agenda—effective tutoring that increases student achievement.
- Built the capacity of eighteen organizations to better serve students and more effectively use resources by providing high-quality professional development, technical assistance, tutor training, and volunteer recruitment.
- Provided a shared measurement system that allows them to measure the impact of tutoring citywide while identifying proven practices that can be scaled throughout the partnership.
- Evaluated results through a contract with Child Trends to conduct an independent evaluation on the impact of tutoring on student achievement in partnership with Greater Twin Cities United Way and SPPS. Founded in 1979, Child Trends is a Washington, DC–based nonprofit, nonpartisan research center that studies children of all stages of development.

In 2013, the Tutoring Partnership's three main goals were to raise student achievement, improve tutoring program quality, and increase the quality of tutors through training. The SPPS Foundation's work with the Tutoring Partnership has resulted in two exciting opportunities, a national project with the David P. Weikart Center for Youth Program Quality and the federal Social Innovation Fund grant through Greater Twin Cities United Way.

The Weikart Center for Youth Program Quality is nationally renowned for developing and implementing the Youth Program Quality Assessment (YPQA). The YPQA is a validated instrument designed to evaluate the quality of youth programs and identify staff training needs. It has been used in community organizations, schools, camps, and places where youths work, have fun, and learn with adults.

In partnership with the Weikart Center, the SPPS Foundation secured $40,000 from Youthprise for a project to develop and field test a supplemental quality-assessment tool specific to tutoring. The Academic Skill Building Program Quality Assessment allows youth programs to measure the quality of academic interventions and use the assessment data to make tangible improvements.

In 2013 the SPPS Foundation was also named a recipient and partner with Generation Next as a Social Innovation Fund (SIF) subgrantee. The SIF subgrant leverages $300,000 annually for the work of the Tutoring Partnership and its community partners while significantly increasing the rigor of its evaluation efforts.

Generation Next is based on the belief that children of all socioeconomic backgrounds should be well prepared for success in the twenty-first century. Its mission is to accelerate educational achievement dramatically from early childhood through early career through an aligned partnership of community stakeholders. The SIF subgrant allows the SPPS Foundation to increase its support for Tutoring Partners and focus on two Generation Next goal areas—reading by third grade and mathematics by eighth grade.

The SPPS Foundation contends that a best-practice tutoring program uses systematic evaluation to assess its impact on student outcomes and inform continuous improvement. The SPPS Foundation (2013) recommends the following:

A Culture of Evaluation. A best-practice tutoring program effectively serves the needs of students by building a culture of evaluation. A tutoring program builds such a culture by involving its staff in the evaluation process. This involvement increases the likelihood that tutoring personnel use the results to implement necessary changes. Most important, a culture of evaluation enables an organization to be accountable and clear to its stakeholders.

The SPPS Foundation suggests the following strategies to build a culture of evaluation:

1. Create a participatory process that is grounded in the context of respective communities.

    a. Involve program personnel and stakeholders in the evaluation process.
    b. Have personnel and stakeholders regularly review, discuss, and act on evaluation findings.
    c. Encourage board members and top leadership to own and act on evaluation findings.
    d. Identify challenges and opportunities in the community that would impact the evaluation.
    e. Be transparent with staff and stakeholders throughout the evaluation process.
    f. Use evaluation as an ongoing function of management and leadership by incorporating staff assessments into the evaluation process.

2. Create an internal evaluation structure that translates evaluation results into action steps for program improvement.

    a. Train staff on how to interpret and use evaluation findings.
    b. Develop quality-improvement teams that meet regularly to discuss results and suggest action steps.

3. Train staff and volunteers on evaluation and data collection.

    a. Intentionally train tutors on recording information about tutoring sessions.

      b. Explain the importance and purpose of evaluation.
      c. Show how the information will be used.

4. Train staff to use data properly and appropriately.

      a. Follow data privacy standards and regulations.
      b. Use data according to its intended application.

5. Develop an evaluation budget.

      a. Allocate specific funds to evaluation efforts.
      b. Include an evaluation line item in grant proposals.
      c. Estimate about 10 to 15 percent of programming costs for evaluation.

Evaluation as an Improvement Tool. Evaluation is a systematic tool that strengths programs as they develop and grow. Furthermore, evaluation provides personnel with the opportunity to discuss program challenges and participate in the process of finding potential solutions.

The following strategies can help a tutoring program use evaluation as a continuous quality improvement tool:

1. Track student progress to determine program impact.

      a. Use standardized test data to measure student academic achievement.
      b. Implement regular assessments, for example pre- and posttesting and surveys, to track the academic progress of students.
      c. Track student, tutor, and intervention data to use in the evaluation.

2. Build data collection systems that ensure accurate and consistent reporting.

   a. Ensure system is accessible to staff and volunteers.
   b. Collect information that is relevant and useful.
   c. Keep the purpose and use in mind when developing collection tools and databases.
   d. Use an electronic document or database to record important information.
   e. Designate a staff member who is responsible for entering the information regularly.

3. Measure the implementation of program practices.

   a. Implement a process for gathering feedback on the quality of the program, for example, through surveys and interviews.
   b. Facilitate internal and/or external observations of the model and its implementation.
   c. Use a quality-assessment tool to determine where the program can improve.

4. Use multiple techniques and data collection tools to address evaluation questions.

   a. Use both qualitative and quantitative methods.
   b. Employ a variety of data collection techniques, for example surveys, focus groups, assessments, and interviews.

Logic Model and Evaluation Plan. To effectively create a culture of evaluation and use evaluation results for improvement, a program must implement both a logic model and an evaluation plan as key tools in its internal evaluation structure. Logic models are flowcharts that depict program components. Logic models provide the framework for programs to connect essential elements by visually presenting the activities and goals of the program. These models can include any number of program elements showing the development of a program from theory to activities and outcomes. The process of developing logic models serves to clarify program elements and expectations for stakeholders.

An evaluation plan is the tool that allows programs to determine how questions that are formulated by stakeholders will be answered and who will be responsible for specific tasks. When a program evaluation plan has a long-term focus and is implemented with fidelity, it empowers an organization to use evaluations to reach its overall goals.

The following strategies facilitate the logic model and evaluation process:

1. Use a logic model template to connect program activities to expected outcomes.

    a. Ensure that program activities align with desired outcomes.
    b. Describe program outputs (the extent to which activities are implemented).
    c. Include short-term outcomes, interim outcomes, and long-term outcomes.
    d. Determine program assumptions that link activities to desired outcomes.

2. Develop an evaluation plan.

a. Use the program logic model as a guide for the evaluation plan.
b. Decide whether to evaluate needs, processes, and/or outcomes.
c. Determine the central questions for the evaluation.
d. Identify methods and tools needed to answer evaluation questions.

To make evaluations an integral part of a tutoring program, they must become a part of all processes and structures. A program must therefore be designed with evaluation in mind, and data must be collected on an ongoing basis and used to improve the program continually. The development and implementation of a good evaluation system has many benefits, such as the following:

- Better understanding of target audiences' needs and how to meet their needs
- Design of objectives that are more achievable and measurable
- Monitoring progress toward objectives more effectively and efficiently
- Increased learning from evaluations
- Increasing a program's productivity and effectiveness

The SPPS Foundation is committed to measuring its impact on students, teachers, and schools. It believes that evaluating its programs allows the organization to serve its communities more effectively.

Tutoring is one way the SPPS Foundation demonstrates its commitment to the success of students in SPPS. In Saint Paul, tutoring is proven to be a learning support for many students. When implemented to the highest standards, tutoring supplements learning, reinforces and builds skills for achievement, enhances a student's connection to the classroom, and increases student motivation.

The SPPS Foundation strives to increase student success and improve the quality of tutoring by providing professional development, tutor training, and technical assistance to tutoring programs. To support this capacity building, the SPPS Foundation has created a research-based guide that is centered on best practices for tutoring programs for its partners and the wider community of community organizations. The guide contains evaluation approaches that tutoring programs at any level of development can use to better match program delivery to the needs of students to create a lasting and powerful impact.

Appendix B contains a list of the Foundation's best practices for tutoring programs. Additional information about the SPPS Foundation is available at http://sppsfoundation.org/.

826 NATIONAL

In 2002, award-winning educator Nínive Calegari and award-winning author Dave Eggers founded 826 National in San Francisco. It is a network of nonprofit organizations. 826 National is the center of the 826 network. It provides strategic leadership, administration, and other resources to ensure the success of its network of eight writing and tutoring centers. As of 2014, 826 National had eight centers in the United States located in San Francisco, New York City, Los Angeles, Seattle, Chicago, Ann Arbor/Detroit/Ypsilanti, Boston, and Washington, DC.

826 National centers offer free after-school tutoring for students ages six through eighteen. In the 2012–2013 school year, 826 programs served 29,449 students across eight states. In addition to 826 National's eight centers, more than thirty cities in the United States

and twelve international cities provide 826-inspired programming to students and schools in their communities.

The 826 National Model is as follows:

Commitment to Literacy. 826 National chapters provide students with high-quality, engaging, and hands-on literary programs that empower students to develop their creative and expository writing skills. 826 National asserts that it engages students in interdisciplinary learning using writing and creativity from personal narratives to poetry, to enrich and expand upon students' studies in school.

Project-Based Learning. Students at 826 National can become published authors. 826 National chapters publish hundreds of pieces of students' work, to celebrate students' hard work and showcase their results.

Third Place. 826 National believes that its inviting spaces create a third place. The concept of a *third place* was introduced by sociologist Ray Oldenburg in 1989 and later in his 1997 and 1999 books, *The Great Good Place.* The *third place,* also referred to as *third space,* is the concept of a community building. *Third place* refers to social surroundings separate from the two usual social environments of home and the workplace (for students, school). Oldenburg contends that third places are important for civil society, democracy, civic engagement, and establishing feelings of a sense of place. *Third places* are environments that offer friendship and a sense of community.

The 826 National *third places* are its writing and tutoring centers. These places welcome students through a storefront with a whimsical theme, such as superheroes or pirates. Oldenburg believes that third places are exciting, fun, and safe learning environments separate from home and school. The 826 National *third places* take away any perceived stigma that surrounds going to a tutoring center. For example, the storefront for 826 National in New York City is the Brooklyn Superhero Supply Company, and the storefront for 826 National in Washington, DC, is The Museum of Unnatural History.

Volunteer and Community Involvement. 826 National makes known that the force behind its efforts is attributable to its vast, dedicated, and hard-working network of volunteers and community members. Working together, they offer individualized attention to students, extend their reach, and ensure the quality of their efforts and their students' experiences.

Teacher and Classroom Support. 826 National's goal is to be a resource to teachers through field trips, in-school programs, and specialized workshops.

The founders of 826 National acknowledge that class sizes, compressed scheduling, and other demands sometimes prevent teachers from undertaking all the assignments they desire with students. 826 National therefore bridges the gap and provides volunteers to assist students with in-school writing projects and classroom support.

The 826 National mission is based on the understanding that great leaps in learning can happen with one-on-one attention and that strong writing skills are fundamental to future success. 826 National's after-school tutoring program provides students individualized help with homework up to four days a week, regardless of the subject. After homework is completed, students are encouraged to spend thirty minutes reading with their tutors, and a final hour is dedicated to writing.

In the summer, many 826 National centers cater principally to English language learners. Research suggests that English language learners (ELLs) will comprise more than 40 percent of elementary and secondary students by 2030 in the United States (Thomas & Collier, 1997). 826 National, therefore, endeavors to cater exclusively to ELLs in the summertime, when children are away from school and learning diminishes. The endeavor allows ELLs to obtain the needed assistance to improve their English skills to achieve success in school.

826 National uses a combination of external evaluation, objective assessment, and program surveys given to students, parents, teachers, and volunteers. The combination allows stakeholders to learn more about 826 National's effectiveness and scope. After the 2011–2012 school year, 826 National also compiled the results of its first chapter-wide assessment of writing skills. Hammill and Larsen (2009) "The Test of Written Language-Fourth Edition (TOWL-4)" is an objective measure created by external researchers that evaluates writing abilities before and after involvement in 826 National programs.

The results compiled from 190 students indicated that there was an increase of 8 percent in students' contextual convention abilities (for example, noun-verb agreement and punctuation) and 13 percent in story composition skills (for example, vocabulary, prose, and plot). Surveys revealed that 826 National positively affects all areas, from building academic skills to fostering excitement about learning.

In February 2013, the first strategic plan for 826 National was approved. 826 National has identified these four strategic priorities for its staff and board for the fiscal years 2014–2016:

- Research and evaluate programs to assess impact, document results, and ensure the quality and consistency of core programs.

- Promote the 826 National brand on a national level. Communicate and advocate for the importance of writing and creativity in the national arena.
- Strengthen internal operations to fortify existing sites and prepare for realistic expansion.
- Create a robust and sustainable fundraising strategy to support its national office and network and raise funds from diverse national sources that boost local efforts.

826 National 2012–2013 impact results reveal the following:

- Ninety-two percent of after-school-tutored students reported that after a year of after-school tutoring, they felt confident in their ability to complete their homework assignments.
- Ninety-two percent of parents of after-school-tutored students said that their child's writing skills improved with the help of 826 National.
- One hundred percent of teachers collaborated with during the in-schools projects said their students were engaged and challenged during the project and that 826 National is a good resource for teachers.
- Ninety-four percent of volunteers giving time to 826 National said they would recommend 826 National as a volunteer opportunity to their friends.
- Eighty-five percent of students who participated in 826 National in-schools projects said that volunteer tutors from 826 National helped them increase their confidence about writing.
- Ninety-eight percent of field-trip teachers said that 826 National field trips are a valuable and unique learning opportunity.

826 National's on-site and in-school programs are based on the idea that if creativity is celebrated, it engages and assists children. The 826 National office was established in 2008 to serve the growing network of chapters by maintaining the brand, developing evaluation systems, coordinating national press and marketing initiatives, building a base of national supporters, ensuring programmatic quality and consistency, and overseeing replication of the 826 model. Additional information for 826 National is available at http://www.826national.org.

BUILDING EDUCATED LEADERS FOR LIFE (BELL)

Building Educated Leaders for Life (BELL) is a national nonprofit organization that serves scholars in kindergarten through grade eight in literacy and mathematics instruction in the United States. Led by Earl Martin Phalen and Andrew Lamar Carter Jr. in the early 1990s, a group of students at Harvard University in the Harvard Law School worked with parents, teachers, and experts to transform the lives of children who were unable to read, write, or perform mathematics operations at grade-level proficiency. Harvard University originated BELL in Boston and incorporated it in 1992. BELL is named in honor of Professor Derrick A. Bell Jr., a Harvard Law professor.

BELL refers to its students as scholars, because they are recognized for their tremendous potential to excel. BELL's after-school program outcomes are measured against three major goals for scholars: improved academic performance, enhanced self-concept and self-efficacy, and increased social skills. Evaluation activities by the BELL after-school program also assessed parent engagement and satisfaction with the program.

The BELL educational after-school program integrates best practices in academic tutoring, enrichment, and evaluation. The program aims to improve scholar's academic performance, self-concept, and social/community skills. The program provides a thirty-week extended-day tutoring program for African American and Latino boys. It offers rigorous literacy and mathematics instruction, social enrichment activities, mentoring relationships, and parental engagement.

Since BELL's inception, the after-school programs have served more than 100,000 scholars in schools throughout the United States. During the 2013–2014 school year, BELL's after-school program served 12,828 scholars. BELL works in California, Maryland, Massachusetts, New Jersey, New York, North Carolina, and Ohio, and through a partnership with the Young Men's Christian Association of the United States and its national network, BELL also serves scholars in Alabama, Colorado, Connecticut, Florida, Minnesota, Texas, and Washington, DC (BELL, 2014).

BELL's strategic partners are the National Summer Learning Association, New York Life Foundation, Target, Walmart, and WilmerHale LLP. BELL's after-school program is based on strong partnerships with schools and delivers small-group academic instruction, mentorship, a wide range of enrichment activities, and community engagement. The BELL after-school program expands learning time during the school year to increase scholars' master academic skills and ensure they succeed in school.

BELL works diligently with principals and teachers to design and deliver after-school programs that align with school-day learning and priorities. BELL's after-school program starts with a healthy snack followed by rigorous, small-group tutoring led by certified teachers and highly trained tutors. BELL's staff uses research-based curricula aligned to the Common Core standards and applies data from computer-adaptive assessments to differentiate instruction and develop individualized learning plans, according to scholars' unique learning needs.

BELL lists these five principles present in each of its after-school programs:

- High expectations—Students are referred to as scholars. Scholars are expected to attend regularly and fully complete programs. Scholars are treated with respect.
- Partnerships for success—Program themes, content, and goals align with the priorities of school and district partners. BELL staffs are involved in the school environment and develop strong relationships with school leaders and faculty. Parents are esteemed as partners in their scholars' learning.
- Exceptional learning environment—BELL believes that well-trained leaders produce an exceptional learning environment for scholars. BELL programs are well structured and organized. Scholars learn in a small-group setting that is supportive and adaptive to their learning needs. BELL staff continually monitors program metrics and improves program quality.
- Teaching excellence—Academic instruction is rigorous and data driven. Differentiation is used to meet individual scholar needs. Staff serves as role models for scholars.
- Relevant and engaging learning experiences—BELL programs enhance scholars' social and emotional learning. Scholars expand their educational horizons through enrichment activities, project-based learning, field trips, and community-service opportunities.

Scholars are exposed to materials and questions that successfully prepare them for twenty-first-century learning.

BELL is also nationally recognized for its rigorous approach to program evaluation. Its evaluation activities are guided, advised, and endorsed by an external, interdisciplinary group, BELL's national Evaluation Advisory Board. The responsibility of the Evaluation Advisory Board is to supervise the application of principles and standards established in the evaluation field.

Evaluation results support scholar achievement; demonstrate program impact to parents, teachers, principals, donors, other partners; and continually strengthen the program quality. BELL's model of applying evaluation data for continuous program improvement has been nationally recognized by the Academy for Educational Development as a best practice in expanded learning programming.

The evaluative questions guiding the outcome measurement process of the BELL after-school programs include the following:

- Did scholars demonstrate improved literacy and math skills?
- Did scholars demonstrate improvement during the school day?
- Did scholars report higher levels of self-esteem?
- Did scholars demonstrate improved social skills?
- Did parents engage in scholars' education?
- Did the program meet parents' expectations?

BELL rigorously evaluates program effectiveness through a series of quantitative and qualitative measures, including pre- and post-program computer-adaptive assessments and standardized diagnostic tests; parent, teacher, and scholar surveys; youth outcome assessments; and portfolio assessment.

At the start of each BELL program, scholars complete a computer-adaptive assessment or a paper-based test to enable BELL's team to identify strengths and weaknesses and develop individualized learning plans. At the end of each BELL program, a second assessment or test quantify scholar learning gains, while a series of scholar, teacher, and parent surveys provide qualitative data about changes in scholars' self-concept and social competency.

The 2012–2013 BELL's after-school evaluation report revealed that scholars increased their percentile rank scores and positive Normal Curve Equivalent (NCE) scores in their programs. Percentile rank scores range from one to ninety-nine. The number fifty represents the middle score and denotes average performance at or near grade level. Percentile rank scores provide a relative measure that compares BELL scholar performance to national norms.

The evaluation report revealed that on average, scholars were underperforming when they first enrolled in BELL after-school programs. On average, scholars entered the after-school program at the 33rd percentile in reading and the 27th in mathematics. After being in a BELL after-school program, scholars increased their percentile rank scores to an average of 37th and 33rd percentiles in reading and mathematics. This information proves that BELL narrowed scholars' achievement gap.

The normal curve equivalent scores indicate that scholars gained new literacy and mathematics skills at a faster rate than their peers during the school year, indicated by a positive NCE score on standardized diagnostic tests. NCE scores show a student's position compared to others in the same grade and tested at the same time of year. A gain in NCE indicates that the student has grown more than the norm group. The average student demonstrates no change, for a NCE score of zero.

The 2013–2014 BELL's after-school impact report indicated that scholars increased their scaled scores in the program. Scaled scores are useful to compare scholar performance over time and are mathematically transformed from one set of numbers, such as a raw score, to another set of numbers to make them comparable. BELL scholars' increased scaled scores suggest that partaking in after-school programs could improve the chances for a positive effect on student achievement.

BELL scholars are targeted because of their underperformance in school. They need to learn at an accelerated rate, to succeed academically, such as demonstrating a positive change in NCE scores. BELL's after-school evaluation report indicates that the program boosts scholars' engagement in learning and academic achievement. BELL's scholars have been known to experience success, gain self-confidence, and be more prepared to succeed in the classroom. Additional information on BELL is available at: http://www.experiencebell.org/.

The Out-of-School Time (OST) Program Research and Evaluation Bibliography published by the Harvard Family Research Project (Harvard Graduate School of Education, 2014) also contains a list of citations for all the out-of-school time program evaluations and research studies that they track. Included in the citation are the BELL Accelerated Learning Summer Program, BELL After-School Instructional Curriculum, and Boys of BELL.

Since 1983, Harvard Family Research Project has helped stakeholders develop and evaluate strategies to promote the well-being of children, families, and their communities. They work primarily within three areas that support children's learning and development—early childhood education, out-of-school time programming, and family and community support in education.

The project focuses national attention on complementary learning. Complementary learning is the knowledge that a systemic approach that integrates school and nonschool supports better ensures that all children have the skills they need to succeed. Access to the Harvard Family Research Project bibliography is available at: http://www.hfrp.org/out-of-school-time/ost-database-bibliography/bibliography?topic=16.

The SPPS Foundation (SPPS), 826 National, and BELL exemplify some of the best-practice after-school tutoring programs. These programs provide stakeholders with hands-on tools that contain practical strategies and resources that are high-quality and evidence-based.

POINTS TO REMEMBER

Tutors serve an important academic and social role and can ensure student success in school. Tutors must, however, remain open, respectful, and honest to their students and build strong interpersonal relationships.

Many researchers have identified effective components of successful tutoring programs that improve the chances for a positive effect on student achievement. These researchers reveal that successful tutoring programs must be intensive, consistent, and structured; use diagnostic/development; have intensive and ongoing training and feedback for tutors; have systematic reflective assessments by tutors of student progress; and provide close coordination with teacher and classroom.

The chapter also lists the National Tutoring Association (2013) Tutor Code of Ethics. This Code of Ethics provides members with opportunities to achieve and maintain high professional standards for tutors and administrators of tutoring programs and services. Some institutions within the last decade have designated one week in October to recognize their tutors by celebrations in the National Tutoring Week and the International Tutor Appreciation Week.

Tutoring has been greatly influenced by tutoring programs such as the Reading Recovery, which also contains components researchers have identified as effective components of successful tutoring programs. The SPPS Foundation, 826 National, and BELL are also examples of organizations that strive to institute best-practice tutoring programs. These organizations contain several effective components of successful tutoring programs. They have strategies and resources that can be replicated by any tutoring programs in any setting and at any level of development. These best-practice tutoring programs all work to increase student success by implementing and sustaining successful tutoring programs to create a long-lasting and positive effect on students' academic accomplishment.

It is important to note that effective tutoring does not just happen. Successful programs must be planned, implemented, monitored, and modified systematically. On the whole, successful tutoring programs benefit students and let them face the world and others with openness and confidence.

Chapter Four

Technology and Online Tutoring

This chapter discusses the technology of interactive learning and the Net Generation, along with an overview of online tutoring. The chapter also provides a practical example of a prominent United States–based online tutoring organization, Smarthinking Incorporated. In addition, the chapter focuses on SRI International, Worcester Polytechnic Institute, and the University of Maine, institutions charged with the evaluation of the effectiveness of online mathematics tutoring. Further, the chapter highlights two international online tutoring institutions, Tutoring Australasia (core service, Yourtutor), Australia-based, and TutorVista, India-based. The chapter ends with a list of some major private global tutoring companies covered in a report by Global Industry Analysts Incorporated, a leading publisher of market research worldwide.

TECHNOLOGY OF INTERACTIVE LEARNING AND THE NET GENERATION

Psychologist Mihaly Csikszentmihalyi (1990) contends that computer technology has had a tremendous potential to replicate moments of optimum flow or mindfulness. Csikszentmihalyi asserts that optimum flow occurs when alienation gives way to involvement, enjoyment replaces boredom, helplessness turns into a feeling of control, and psychic energy works to reinforce the sense of self, instead of being lost in the service of external goals. He also affirmed that the job of educators was to replicate moments of optimum flow. Several learning theorists also support the use of technology, namely computers, in learning institutions.

In 1998, Don Tapscott communicated in his book *Growing up Digital: The Rise of the Net Generation* that America was in a digital era of learning. Tapscott argued that a transformation in learning was taking place from what he labeled *broadcast* learning to *interactive learning*. He observed that students were no longer satisfied with being the passive receivers of the traditional teaching process. Students wanted to discover learning by becoming interactive with the learning process.

Tapscott further communicated that the Net Generation of students processed information and learned differently from the generation before it. The Net Generation from zero to age twenty embraced interactive media such as the Internet, CD-ROM, and video games. These new media at that time, Tapscott contended, offered great promise for a new model of learning that was based on discovery and participation. He found that the Net Generation of students was exceptionally curious, self-reliant, smart, focused, and able to adapt and had high self-esteem and global orientation.

Tapscott also stressed that demographically speaking, not only was the Net Generation the greatest challenge to cultural supremacy, but technologically speaking, there also was a transformation in the way children gathered, accepted, and retained information. In 1998, Tapscott stressed that if computers were harnessed by schools, they would become a tremendous force to promote learning.

Today technology is virtually everywhere. Students are bombarded by technology and surrounded by it in schools, homes, and communities. Technology has become a part of the educational process and enhances the way students learn. Technology investments for children not only benefit communities and businesses, but also enhance economic vitality (Nelson-Royes, 2012). The Internet, an instrument of innovation in education, makes online learning and tutoring practical and cost effective. The next generations of learners will be exposed to technology at an early age and will certainly meet and surpass the Net Generation's expectations of educational standards.

ONLINE TUTORING

Online tutoring is one of the fastest growing educational settings in the United States, and it is also implemented internationally. Online teaching and learning is used increasingly. Currently there is a shift from paper-based materials to electronic materials and from face-to-face support to online support. Online tutoring is the process of tutoring where tutors and students are separated by space and sometimes time. Further, online tutoring allows students to work with a tutor using an instant-messenger-like text chat and a shared whiteboard. This interactive graphical chat tool allows tutors and students to communicate complex concepts in real time. Other advanced online systems offer features such as multiple whiteboards, graphing tools, file sharing, and web-page sharing back and forth.

Online tutoring allows students to meet with a tutor anytime, from any computer, without making an appointment. It delivers one-on-one help up to twenty-four hours a day, seven days a week.

Drop-in live sessions allow students to ask written questions or submit written assignments such as essays or reports for feedback, usually deliverable in twenty-four hours. Some online tutoring systems record their tutoring sessions so students can review them later. The spontaneous nature of online tutoring allows students to be mentally stimulated and get immediate instruction before they become discouraged.

On-demand assistance between an online tutor and student can occur by text, Skype, FaceTime, and online whiteboard. The whiteboard is a real-time interactive learning environment where both the tutor and student use text, colors, and graphical tools to discuss ideas and solve problems (Hewett, 2006). Specialized mathematical and language tools enable students to input data easily on a whiteboard, even fractions and accented characters.

Educational Tutorial Services (2013), a member of the Education Industry Association—an industry leader in academic tutoring programs that serve students from all backgrounds, indicates that the following items make online tutoring meaningful:

- The right tools or features. For students that are visual, a method that allows the student to see what the tutor is teaching is more practical. A whiteboard feature therefore presents a good option, because it allows tutors to illustrate their explanations. On the other hand, if a student learns best by listening, select a tool that allows the student to listen to what the tutor is teaching, for instance a video chat between a tutor and student.
- Self-discipline. Online learning and teaching takes place in a computer-generated classroom, so no one physically supervises or ensures that students give full attention to what is being communicated.

- Clarification and feedback from the tutor. Online tutoring is a computer-generated experience, making it difficult for tutors to read students' body language. As a result, tutors are sometimes unable to determine if a student is confused or comprehends what is being conveyed. For that reason, when students are doubtful, clarification and feedback between tutors and students become valued learning tools.

When the above considerations are met, online tutoring allows students to gain academic skills required to succeed in the changing technological landscape of education in the twenty-first century.

Online tutoring has emerged as a popular form of supplemental education for students around the world. In the United States, online tutoring can be used for academic assistance from kindergarten through college level or for preparation for the graduate record examination, graduate management admission test, law school admission test, scholastic aptitude test, American college testing, or test of English as a foreign language. The best tutoring institutions have educators available to work with any student, regardless of the student's need or knowledge level. Even students with learning disabilities and other disadvantages can get custom-designed tutoring assignments to achieve their learning goals.

Smarthinking Incorporated

Smarthinking Incorporated is a prominent Washington, DC–based organization that provides technology and training to help schools and institutions offer exceptional online academic support to their students. Cofounded by Burck Smith and Christopher Gergen in 1999, Smarthinking is now a member of Pearson—one of the world's leading education and publication companies. According to

Maeroff (2003), Chediak (2005), and Powers and Hewett (2008), the creation of Smarthinking was a logical extension of Smith's (1999) research on the economic and organizational challenges that faced higher education.

Smarthinking was founded on the premise that professional educators could deliver educational services by means of the Internet. Today Smarthinking is a premier provider of research-based, research-proven online tutoring. Smarthinking's numerous online tutors around the globe help more than 1,000 universities, colleges, high schools, libraries, government agencies, textbook publishers, and other education providers. Smarthinking endeavors to increase student achievement, increase retention, and improve learning. Smarthinking's online tutoring services are based on key research findings on effective tutoring and professional development, an essential component of successful tutoring programs, as discussed in chapter 3.

Academic directors and coordinators in the education department manage the external workforce of online tutors at Smarthinking. The external workforce consists of hundreds of online tutors who are veteran educators. Ninety percent of these educators have advanced degrees in their field and average more than nine years of teaching or tutoring experience. Tutors can be college faculty, graduate students, high school teachers, or retired educators. Smarthinking is distinguished by high-quality instruction provided by its global network of more than 2,000 trained veteran educators.

Smarthinking works to facilitate a culture of professional reflection and consistent quality among its tutors. All tutors must successfully complete a real-time, online training program that focuses on both technological skill and online instructional practices. Each academic area is led by one of Smarthinking's subject-area coordinators, all of whom are former college professors and experts in their disciplines. Smarthinking's certification program consists of a combination of self-paced online modules and interactive sessions with veteran tutors and is regularly evaluated for quality and consistency.

During the course of an academic year, Smarthinking holds ongoing development exercises for its tutors. Tutors also communicate with each other regularly through communication tools such as instant messaging. These communications are regulated by lead tutors and academic coordinators. Ongoing communication provides opportunities for tutors to engage in continuing conversations about their practices and to build a sense of community with colleagues.

Upon completion of Smarthinking's program, tutors must demonstrate competence in specific content areas and online communication and instruction, as well as an understanding of the values that drive Smarthinking's practice. The education department at Smarthinking engages tutors in ongoing evaluation and professional development exercises. Academic coordinators undertake formal biweekly evaluations of tutor performance followed by debriefing sessions, as well as less formal daily monitoring of tutoring activities. These reviews focus on specific challenges and complexities of working with a diverse student population in an online learning environment.

The primary technological tool at Smarthinking is a proprietary virtual whiteboard. Synchronous and asynchronous online tutoring is provided for several general education and degree-specific courses for secondary and postsecondary education. Synchronous and asynchronous whiteboard interactions between tutors and students are archived and available for students to review at any time.

The archived interactions ensure the analysis of quality control and the implementation of standards.

While synchronous tutoring allows students to interact with online tutors in real time by the use of a whiteboard technology, asynchronous tutoring allows students to ask questions offline or submit essay drafts for a tutor critique. Students can access online tutoring services from home, school, libraries, or any other Internet-connected location. Services are provided twenty-four hours a day and seven days a week. Students who want to plan ahead can schedule a thirty-minute appointment with a tutor of their choice.

Smarthinking is not limited by its geographic area, but is able to choose the most highly qualified professionals to deliver services efficiently across various educational institutions. Smarthinking provides the technology for schools to staff their own online tutoring centers. It also licenses its technology platform to clients and provides training and consulting on the delivery of online tutoring programs. Furthermore, a school can also pool its tutors with Smarthinking certified tutors to create a comprehensive online tutoring structure. Nevertheless, if Smarthinking's access is not available through an institution, an independent student or an individual can purchase its services independently.

Research indicates that online tutoring fosters student achievement in various subjects and improves student retention. In an independent study conducted by Broward Community College (BCC) in Florida (2005), researchers found that students using Smarthinking's online tutoring service in their online writing lab had higher pass rates than nonusers. Broward Community College (now Broward College), is a diverse, multi-campus community college in Broward County, Florida. BCC is the second largest community college in Florida and is ranked in the top eleven U.S. public four-year institutions with the lowest tuition in Florida.

To determine the effectiveness of Smarthinking, researchers identified 451 Smarthinking students in a population of 10,882 students enrolled in BCC's most popular courses in mathematics and English. The college compared the course pass rates of students using Smarthinking to the course pass rates of students who did not use the service. In every course, students who used Smarthinking had significantly higher pass rates than nonusers. The results were found to be most dramatic in mathematics, a subject where students typically struggle.

According to Dr. Larry Calderon, president of BCC (2005a) Smarthinking enables them to provide students with the academic assistance they need to succeed and also improves BCC student pass rates. Calderon confirms that higher pass rates lead to higher student retention rates, which lead to greater revenues. As a result of the study, BCC made Smarthinking available to every student.

Table 4.1 shows the Broward Community College pass rate comparison: Students using Smarthinking and All Other Students.

Jane Calfee (2007) stated that students earned significantly higher grades as a result of using online tutoring. In 2008, Smarthinking launched Voice over Internet Protocol (VoIP) sessions in the Spanish language with plans for development in other subjects to accommodate a variety of student learning styles and abilities.

VoIP is a method and group of technologies for the delivery of voice communications and multimedia sessions over the Internet. Smarthinking endeavors to provide personalized learning solutions that improve success and retention for all students.

Table 4.1. Broward Community College Pass Rate Comparison: Students Using Smarthinking and All Other Students

Course	Smarthinking Students	All Other Students	Smarthinking Difference
Composition 1	76%	66%	+10%
Elementary Algebra	52%	36%	+16%
Intermediate Algebra	50%	40%	+10%
Developmental Writing	76%	57%	+19%
College Algebra	58%	46%	+12%
Pre-Calculus	81%	59%	+22%
College Trigonometry	88%	68%	+20%
Introduction to Statistics	71%	63%	+8%

Source: Broward Community College. (2005). *Does tutoring help? A comparison of Smarthinking-tutored and non-tutored students' grades college-wide*. Fort Lauderdale, FL: Broward Community College. Retrieved from: http://cit.westfield.ma.edu/smarthinking/pdf/smarthinking_proven.pdf.

SRI International, Worcester Polytechnic Institute, and the University of Maine

SRI International, Worcester Polytechnic Institute (WPI), and the University of Maine received a $3.5 million award from the Institute of Education Sciences at the U.S. Department of Education to evaluate the effectiveness of an online tutoring system for mathematics homework. The four-year research study began April 1, 2012, and ends March 31, 2016 (U.S. Department of Education, 2012). Maine was chosen to conduct the study because its students are assigned laptops to take home and use for homework.

Homework has been an active area of study among American education researchers for decades. For example Hagan (1927) compared the effects of homework with the effects of in-school supervised study on the achievement of eleven- and twelve-year-olds. Homework can be defined as any task assigned by schoolteachers intended for students to carry out during nonschool hours (Cooper, 1989). Homework plays a vital role in developing student motivation and achievement.

The study is the first gold-standard-quality study in the United States on the use of online homework in middle school mathematics learning. It involves about 2,500 seventh-grade students and teachers in more than fifty schools throughout Maine using WPI's ASSISTments system. In 2013, eighth-grade mathematics students were included in the study. The eighth-grade addition is a two-year study also funded by the U.S. Department of Education and in collaboration with WPI, SRI International, and the University of Maine. Results will be measured using the Common Core State Standards (Maine Department of Education, 2013) discussed in the preface.

ASSISTments aims to transform homework by giving students instant feedback and tutoring adapted to their individual needs. Schools who participate in the study receive free use of ASSISTments for four years, and their homework assignments are customized to their textbooks. ASSISTments are free online formative assessment and tutoring platforms in mathematics developed by Neil Heffernan, coprincipal investigator, and colleagues at WPI.

Assistance and assessment are integrated in ASSISTments, and the system learns more about the students' abilities each time they work on the website. It provides tutored, practice problem-solving support for students and cognitive diagnostic reports to teachers. It supports students' mathematics homework completion and facilitates differentiated instruction.

Research at WPI is known to have a definitely applied focus that results in new knowledge and innovations and technological advances that address major challenges of society. The faculty members and students engage in leading-edge research across a broad range of disciplines. WPI's historic strength in interdisciplinary research and education is also known to provide it with an important advantage.

SRI International, a nonprofit research and development organization, performs sponsored research and development for governments, businesses, and foundations. SRI International conducts education research in three main areas: education reform, education policy, and the application of technology to improve education. One of SRI International missions is to improve teaching and learning by conducting research on the innovative design, use, and assessment of interactive learning environments.

SRI International is based on the tenet that although homework is important, traditional ways of doing homework do not support students who need extra help. Most important, the company works toward making homework a better learning experience, with students receiving instant feedback and online tutoring, as well as specially organized "practice-makes-perfect" sessions. In 2011, Nelson-Royes and Reglin indicated in their study of an after-school tutoring program that practice makes perfect and that educators perceived that more practice generated greater success and improvement.

According to Heffernan, early small studies showed solid learning gains for students who use ASSISTments and led to its implementation in other schools (PR Newswire Association, 2012). The four-year research study compares ASSISTments to existing ways of doing mathematics homework. Researchers in the study continue to examine whether ASSISTments is effective and investigate the teaching practices that are central to increased learning using the system. Researchers look especially at whether students who previously struggled in mathematics benefit from online homework tutoring and how these benefits vary, depending on the students' socioeconomic status.

Benefits for students and teachers using ASSISTments include the following:

- Time saved on homework management
- Instant feedback
- Automatic grading
- Online support through hints and examples
- Useful reports
- Differentiated instruction options
- Collaborative learning community

As in any successful tutoring programs, teachers in the study are provided with professional development on how to use ASSISTments reports as formative assessment tools. Professional development allows teachers to learn how to use online homework and reports to differentiate instruction to meet students' individual needs.

Teachers receive daily customized reports on their students' nightly progress. These customized reports are valuable tools to teachers. The reports inform teachers of their students' homework completion status and problem areas and allow teachers to adapt their instruction accordingly, to better suit their students' needs. Reports also inform teachers about changes in classroom routines and the use of differentiated instruction based on group- and individual-level student information.

According to Baker et al. (2004) and Walonoski and Heffernan (2006), ASSISTments communicates more about students' activities than their performance. These researchers indicate that it exposes students' unusual behavior, such as students who make more attempts and request more hints than other students in the classroom. They point out that this information indicates that some students do not take ASSISTments seriously or try to gain an advantage over other users.

In 2011, before the SRI International, WPI, and the University of Maine study, a mathematics ASSISTments online tutor for middle school mathematics was developed with funding from a coprincipal investigator Heffernan National Science Foundation grant. The grant amount of $711,609, from June 1, 2011, to 2014, predicted STEM career choice from computational indicators of student engagement within middle school mathematics classes.

The acronym STEM stands for Science, Technology, Engineering, and Mathematics. These four disciplines are integrated in teaching to promote real-world experience, teamwork, and the authentic application of technology. STEM also promotes discovery, problem-based learning, and project-based learning and is supported by the National Science Foundation and the U.S. Department of Education.

The grant provides individualized mathematics tutoring services to 135 eighth and eleventh graders in Minneapolis during the 2013–2014 academic year. Tutoring services were designed to meet the participating students' unique challenges in the mathematics content studied. The grant supported the Prepare2Nspire program, which prepares underrepresented students to succeed on grade-level, high-stakes mathematics exams and stimulates them to continue their study of mathematics.

Other institutions, such as the University of Minnesota STEM Education Center, have also been recipients of a $300,000 College Ready grant from the Great Lakes Higher Education Guaranty Corporation. Its College Ready grants support programs that actively prepare more students to enroll and succeed in college-level courses. The tutoring, time, attention, and skill-building activities the institution provides through qualified educators and trained tutors give students expanded options for college and increased opportunities for lifelong achievement.

On the whole, the SRI International, WPI, and the University of Maine study measures the benefit to students' mathematics achievement from online homework. It also looks at improvement on required state tests and against national standards and supports components of formative assessment. Feedback is provided to students instantaneously. Teachers receive feedback in the form of user-friendly item reports, and parents receive feedback from automated e-mails and detailed reports.

In 2009, Mendicino et al. indicated that web-based homework assistance was already popular in colleges and had thousands of student users. Some of the systems included Blackboard (www.blackboard.com), WebAssign (www.webassign.com), MasteringPhysics (www.masteringphysics.com), WeBWorK (http://webwork.rochester.edu), and WebCT (www.webct.com). Mendicino et al. indicated, however, that kindergarten through grade-twelve homework assistance lagged behind, but that some systems, such as Study Island (www.studyisland.com) and PowerSchool (www.powerschool.com) were gaining popularity among teachers.

Today, with the proliferation of numerous online tutoring institutions, students are allowed the opportunity of online tutoring and homework assistance services. As technology continues to permeate the world, more countries are using online tutoring and homework assistance opportunities for students' academic support. International online tutoring institutions in countries such as Australia and India have become forerunners in online tutoring and homework assistance.

INTERNATIONAL ONLINE TUTORING INSTITUTIONS

Tutoring Australasia (core service, Yourtutor)

Tutoring as a form of instruction is used worldwide, and its effectiveness as an instructional method has been documented extensively. Jack Goodman (2011) reports that overseas research from the previous decade indicates that children who visited libraries were most interested in getting their schoolwork (homework) done and were looking for any help they could acquire.

Homework is not always completed at home and after-school library programs have become a place that helps students with homework. Goodman affirms that the experience of hundreds of public libraries is that children in Australia are no different from those in countries such as the United States, Canada, and the United Kingdom.

An important question reasoned by Mendicino et al. (2009) is this: do students learn more by using computers to do their homework than by doing traditional paper-and-pencil homework? I posed similar questions to Jack Goodman, founder and chief executive officer of Tutoring Australasia, a provider of homework assistance service for public libraries in Australia. The questions and answers received are listed later in this chapter.

Founded in 2003, Tutoring Australasia is an Australian-owned company that provides the only live, one-on-one, on-demand homework support and tutoring services to public, state, and territory libraries, schools, and departments of education (Goodman, 2011). Tutoring Australasia's mission is to overcome socioeconomic and geographic obstacles to learning, making high quality one-on-one tutoring accessible in every community and to help strengthen paths to higher education.

Jack Goodman (2011) in his article titled "New Directions with Existing Resources: Australian and New Zealand Libraries as Career Development Hubs" indicated that Australia and New Zealand's public libraries had the infrastructure and capacity to build on existing youth services, including homework support, to further position themselves as career development hubs.

Today Tutoring Australasia partners with governments, institutions, and whole communities across Australia and New Zealand. Yourtutor, Tutoring Australasia's core service, is known to build capability, confidence, critical thinking skills, independence, and tertiary aspiration, all with measurable outcomes for education leaders.

Yourtutor provides real time, on-demand, one-on-one tutoring in core curriculum subjects: mathematics, science, and English, as well as research and study skills. It uses online tools and hundreds of qualified Australian tutors who are experts in their field. Yourtutor is made available to more than ten million Australian students, and it states that when students get "'stuck,' Yourtutor gets them 'unstuck.'" Daily there are thousands of students around Australia that connect to Yourtutor to get help with homework assignments, projects, and exam revision.

In 2014, the following were questions posed and answers received from Jack Goodman:

- Is online tutoring more effective than more traditional approaches of tutoring?

  Our definition of online tutoring involves a live, one-on-one interaction between a student and a tutor. We connect students as soon as they get stuck doing their homework. We match them to the next available subject expert, usually in a few minutes or less, and assist them to get "unstuck" and move forward with their work. We are thus solving a different problem than traditional tutoring solves. Traditional tutoring normally involves regularly scheduled interactions between a student and tutor. Yourtutor staffs tutors across all core academic subjects, so students can get help with an English essay, a mathematics question, sciences, research skills, business studies, economics, and more.

- Do students learn more using online tools to do their homework than they learn using traditional paper-and-pencil homework?

  There is a place for paper and pencil and a place for technology. Our experience in delivering more than 850,000 live, one-on-one student-tutor interactions is that Yourtutor represents a quantum leap forward in assisting students who are struggling and otherwise likely to give up attempting to learn a challenging concept. Students connect to Yourtutor when they need help with an essay, a lab report, algebra, trigonometry, or a calculus question, and after spending an average of about twenty minutes working with a tutor, students come to an understanding that results in what we call an "aha! moment."

- Why are public libraries so important for homework assistance?

  Public libraries are the number-one after-school destination for high school students in Australia and New Zealand. They are also the largest voluntary membership institutions in Australia, with more than 11 million members, nearly half of Australia's population of 23 million. The primary reason students go to libraries is to get their homework done. Public libraries are free, and students from low socioeconomic backgrounds as well as immigrants and other disadvantaged populations use libraries heavily. Our company's mission is to make the highest quality, one-on-one learning support accessible and affordable to all Australians and New Zealanders, regardless of their geographic, economic, social, or other circumstances. Public libraries therefore represent a perfect fit with our mission, as they are free, learning-focused institutions that seek to meet the educational needs of all community members.

- Why do students need homework assistance?

Students need assistance because learning can be challenging, parents and siblings aren't always available and may not have the knowledge to assist, and Google doesn't have all the answers. For homework to be a useful learning tool, students need to have confidence they can complete it. When students get stuck, they often experience stress, which is a natural but counterproductive emotional response. Yourtutor helps alleviate stress by helping students overcome difficulties, complete their homework, and go to class the following day feeling confident, knowledgeable, and ready to learn more.

The fastest-growing demographic of Yourtutor users is university students and other postsecondary learners. These students often face profound challenges in managing the heavy workloads and high expectations of their lecturers and professors and as a result are at high risk of dropping out. A growing number of tertiary institutions, including universities, pathways colleges, and TAFEs (Technical and Further Education [vocational] institutions) use Yourtutor to support student retention and progression and course completion. We are establishing a growing body of evidence that Yourtutor is a cost-effective and efficient way to have a positive impact on student retention rates while at the same time reducing costs compared to face-to-face learning support centers.

- What age student is the target market?

Our target market is students as young as grade seven—the first year of high school in Australia—through first year of university. We serve students in the final years of primary (elementary) school, and we also work with adult learners, providing literacy, numeracy, and job-readiness skills to people aged twenty and above.

- How are tutors selected?

We go to enormous lengths to recruit, train, and background check the highest quality and most capable Australian and New Zealand subject experts. All our tutors are locally based in Oceania (Australia and New Zealand) and have comprehensive knowledge of the variations in the curricula taught by New South Wales, Victoria, Queensland, and other states. We believe this base is essential to delivering the highest-quality learning support for our students.

Tutor applicants apply online and complete a lengthy application of up to sixteen pages of teaching samples, to demonstrate their subject knowledge. They then go through a one-on-one, multi-hour training program with one of our senior mentor tutors. All tutors are assigned to a mentor who reviews their work and provides training and professional development. New tutors are probationary for their first ninety days and are monitored closely by their mentors to ensure they meet our exacting standards.

- What qualifications do tutors possess?

    Our tutors have PhDs, masters degrees, are certified teachers, and post graduates. They are all experts in their subject fields and have a minimum of two or three years of tutoring experience.

- How do intensity, consistency, and structure work in your service?

    Consistency of quality is critical to the success of Yourtutor. Because students do not choose their tutor, it is vitally important that all our tutors work to the exacting standards we set and deliver the same high-quality experience to all students. This means our tutors are also trained and monitored to deliver the same pedagogically sound interactions with students. Our tutors will never just "give answers." Rather, they identify and crystalize the problem the student has and then work through the problem with the student until the student comes to his or her own understanding.

- What training and feedback do tutors receive?

    Every Yourtutor tutorial is recorded and stored for later retrieval by student, tutor, and the tutor's mentor. In addition, all students are given the option of completing a survey at the end of their interaction, and all tutors are required to complete a similar survey, which includes a personal reflection on the quality of the interaction. Our senior mentor tutors regularly use these surveys and the session recordings to review each tutor's work and provide extended professional development feedback. Mentors provide this feedback by the way of our custom-built mentoring software tool, which provides ready access to session logs and other critical information.

    In addition, during Yourtutor service hours, our service is staffed by a duty manager who is available to assist any tutor who has a question while in session with a student. We also maintain a tutor forum where tutors can review our full policy handbook as well as post questions and share experiences with other tutors.

- What are some of the online technologies used?

We build and maintain all our own technologies used to deliver the Yourtutor experience. All our applications are built using modern web standards, which ensures they are accessible through web browsers such as Google Chrome, Firefox, Safari, and Explorer, as well as mobile operating systems such as iOS and Android. Our online classroom features one-on-one chat; multiple, synchronous whiteboards; and file and website sharing. We have also built a database of more than 10,000 questions, with answers and feedback, across all core-curriculum subjects and correlated to the Australian National Curriculum. Our software engineering and design team is continually upgrading and improving our learning platform to take advantage of the latest technologies as well as the feedback we receive from our clients.

- Do tutors perform any assessments of students' progress?

Tutors provide feedback at the end of each student interaction. This feedback consists of a detailed description of the student's question, as well as a summary of the progress made and the student's responsiveness and learning progress. This information can be shared with the student's teacher or parent, along with a full transcript of the entire tutorial.

- Is there any close coordination with tutors and students' classroom teachers?

Coordination between tutors and classroom teachers occurs when students connect to Yourtutor and share their homework questions or feedback from a teacher with the tutors. In this way

tutors can provide direct and immediate support with questions as well as assistance in understanding and interpreting teachers' feedback on written assignments.
- What are the operating hours of the homework assistance service?

  Yourtutor operates from 3:00 p.m. until midnight, Australian Eastern Standard Time (Sydney time), Sunday through Friday. We are open until 1:00 a.m. during Daylight Savings months to serve students in Western Australia, where Daylight Savings is not observed. We have a brief shutdown period over the Christmas holidays, which coincide with summer vacation for Australian students.
- Do students pay for your tutoring services?

  Depending on how students access Yourtutor, the service may be free to them, they may pay indirectly, or they may pay directly. When accessed through a public library, Yourtutor is free to the end user, just as are nearly all other library services. When students access Yourtutor through their school or university's online homework/learning support center, then the institution may pass along the cost, either directly or indirectly. That is, the cost may be bundled into a technology or other tuition fee, or it may be identified specifically in student fees. In 2015, Tutoring Australasia will begin to offer Yourtutor to families as a private service. We are building the technologies and systems to enable parents and caregivers to purchase access on either a pay-as-you-go basis or by a monthly subscription.
- What are the students' attitudes about the system?

  We have been delivering Yourtutor for ten years, and during that time we have delivered in excess of 850,000 one-on-one learning sessions. We provide students with the opportunity to give us feedback in the form of a brief survey at the end of each session, and students complete the survey about 45 percent of the time. We use these surveys, as well as detailed analyses of session transcripts, to assess the quality of the tuition support we provide and to refine and improve our service continually.

In excess of 90 percent of all students who complete the survey rate their sessions excellent, very good, or good. This rating equates to a Net Promoter Score in excess of 50, an indicator of exceptionally high satisfaction with Yourtutor. In addition, about 90 percent of all students completing the survey indicate that Yourtutor is helping them complete their homework, and that they would recommend the service to their friends. Over the last decade we have collected hundreds of thousands of positive comments in feedback from students completing the free-response portion of the survey.

- Does your service work outside of Australia?

Yourtutor is tailored to meet the needs of students in Australia and New Zealand. It is accessible for students and families in certain other geographies of Southeast Asia, including the Philippines, Indonesia, Singapore, Malaysia, Thailand, and Vietnam.

Goodman says there is a new generation of online tutoring companies in the United States, such as InstaEDU, TakeLessons, HelpHub, WyzAnt, and Tutor Universe. These companies, he says, demonstrate that the market for online tutoring is rapidly developing and growth is accelerating, largely because of mobile technology that puts affordable tablets and mobile devices into the hands of millions of students. In addition, Internet technology continues to improve and makes live, one-on-one learning interactions more intuitive and flexible. More importantly, Goodman recognizes that students, parents, and caregivers are getting more at ease with the concept of live online interactions.

Students worldwide use the Internet for homework help and/or tutoring, and it is accessible at the critical moment of learning need, as Goodman indicates when children get "stuck." International online tutoring/homework help institutions such as Tutoring Australasia shows that students and tutoring/homework help programs in Australia are no different from those in the United States and other countries. Tutoring Australasia's program exhibits effective components of successful tutoring programs that many researchers who have examined multiple tutoring programs have stressed improves the chances for a positive effect on student achievement.

In a trial study conducted in 2007, researchers at Open Universities Australia concluded that students using online tutoring service experienced higher success rates and course completions (DeFazio & Deden, 2008) than students who did not use such services.

TutorVista

TutorVista is one of the leading online tutoring companies in the world, with tutors working across India teaching U.S. students. TutorVista is India-based and founded in 2005 by Krishnan Ganesh, an Indian serial entrepreneur and business executive, and his wife, Meena Ganesh.

In *Times of India* (2011), Ganesh said he started TutorVista to provide affordable education services and content globally. He first thought of the idea of online tutoring when he realized the amount of media debate over the crisis in the U.S. school education system. In 2009, Pearson acquired a minority stake in TutorVista, increasing its holding in 2011 to a controlling position. In 2013 Pearson's complete takeover of TutorVista formed part of a wider plan of building significant education services businesses in fast-growing emerging markets such as India (Abrar, 2013).

Pearson's investment in TutorVista gives it control of the world's largest online tutoring business. As stated earlier in the chapter, Smarthinking Incorporated, a Washington, DC–based organization is also a member of Pearson. The acquisition of TutorVista by Pearson follows investments in nations such as China, Brazil, South Africa, and Nigeria. Pearson's acquisitions are intended to make affordable education services and content occur faster globally and help millions of students achieve their educational goals.

TutorVista is primarily engaged in providing online tutoring to students in North America. Like Smarthinking, TutorVista uses VoIP and online whiteboards to connect tutors in India with students mostly in North America. TutorVista, along with the Manipal Group—a major financial and industrial group in South India—also provides curriculum design, teacher training, technology platforms, and school administration services to schools across India.

The market for tutoring after school in India is about $4 billion. TutorVista has about 1,300 employees across online tutoring, school management, Internet and communication technologies, and test preparation and tuition (Mitra, 2014). In addition, the company employs more than 12,000 India-based educators and helps more than half a million students around the world in twenty-nine countries. Included are more than 20,000 students in the United States and United Kingdom. TutorVista employs more than 3,000 tutors across India. Tutoring is outsourced to India because of India's lower compensation rates.

Tutors in India are well informed about the U.S. kindergarten through grade-twelve state standards and teaching styles as well as the comprehensive materials that were developed to help tutors. Tutors at TutorVista have advanced degrees or at least five years of teaching experience. Furthermore, tutors undergo months of training and pass a rigorous certification process before they become certified.

TutorVista offers the following for its students:

- Individualized one-on-one tutoring
- Twenty-four-hour-a-day, seven-day-a-week tutor availability
- Unlimited tutoring
- Same tutor every time
- Homework/assignment help
- Test preparation
- Detailed report about a student's performance

TutorVista adheres to state curriculum across all subjects and Common Core curriculum for English and mathematics. TutorVista endeavors to be established as the leading technology-enabled education service that provides high-quality online tutoring to students around the world at affordable prices. TutorVista has emerged as a key player in the outsourcing of online tutoring services. The company has grown rapidly, with more than five million online sessions served to students worldwide and with tutors spanning India, Australia, United States, United Kingdom, China, and Southeast Asia.

MAJOR PRIVATE GLOBAL TUTORING COMPANIES

According to Global Industry Analysts (GIA) Incorporated (2014), the private global tutoring market is projected to reach U.S. $196.3 billion by 2020 and will surpass the $152 billion mark in 2015 (Araya, 2012). The GIA states that the reason for the rapid increase is a growing need for academic excellence, increased competition for admission into academic institutions, and a shortage of teaching staff in schools and colleges.

The GIA was founded in 1987 and is a leading worldwide publisher of market research. GIA monitors more than 126,000 companies and 9,500 clients in thirty-six countries, publishes more than 1,300 full-scale research reports, and analyzes more than 40,000 market and technology trends.

The GIA report profiles ninety companies with annual estimates and projections for the period 2013 through 2020. The report provides separate comprehensive analytics for the United States, Canada, Europe, and Asia-Pacific. Some major tutoring companies covered in the GIA (2014) report include the following:

- A Plus All Subjects Tutoring Incorporated
- Building Educated Leaders for Life
- Club Z! Tutoring Services
- Educomp Solutions Limited
- Fleet Tutors
- Huntington Learning Centers Incorporated
- JEI Corporation
- JEI Learning Centers
- Kaplan Incorporated
- Kids "R" Kids International, Incorporated
- Kumon, Learn It Systems
- LearningRx
- Mathnasium Limited Liability Company
- Megastudy Company Limited
- Rocket Learning Incorporated
- Sylvan Learning Incorporated
- The Princeton Review Incorporated

- Tutor Doctor
- Tutor.com Incorporated
- TutorVista Global Private Limited
- Woongjin Thinkbig Company Limited

The GIA comprehensive market research report can be accessed at http://www.strategyr.com/pressMCP-1597.asp.

POINTS TO REMEMBER

Technology and online tutoring is used worldwide by numerous students, and its aim is to enhance a student's overall academic performance. Tutoring is no longer restricted to in-person help. There are many tutoring companies, some of which offer online tutoring to students.

According to Farnham (2013), the online tutoring market in the United States is estimated between $125 and $150 million. The growth is mainly attributable to the inability of the standard education system to address the unique needs of each student (Global Industry Analysts, Incorporated, 2014).

Technology is a driver of change that creates new and different learning settings for students and provides teachers with a richness of instructional approaches. Students' educational achievement has become increasingly important, because of globalization and the expanding demands of a technological society. In 1996, the U.S. Department of Education, in the report "Technological Literacy: A National Priority," stated that technological literacy is not just knowing how to use technology for word processing, spreadsheets, and Internet access. Fundamentally, it is using the powerful learning opportunities afforded by technology to increase learning in academic subjects and to increase students' skills.

Today, many online tutors are using technologies such as whiteboards and video conferencing to interact with their students. Students can also interact with their tutors through e-mail for immediate answers. Students have conveyed that interaction with a tutor over the Internet is less frightening than when the tutor is physically present. Similarly, they are also more at ease asking a tutor questions that they would not ask in school in the presence of their peers. Most important, the twenty-four-hour-a-day, seven-day-a-week support offered through online tutoring may mean the difference between success and failure in school for students who are struggling.

Several public libraries and schools throughout the United States and other countries also offer free access to online tutoring services, usually as homework help. Often these services are accessible from a child's home. Basically, a student with a question on a homework assignment can click on to a library link and log into a tutoring website. The student is then connected with an educator who assists with the homework.

According to PR Newswire Association (2014), colleges and universities are adopting online tutoring to expand their individualized support services to meet the demands of an increasingly older student population. With students having instant access to the best tutors anywhere, online tutoring ensures that students receive the best possible help from expert educators.

The continual advancement of technology and globalization makes online tutoring more real-world. Today, technology and online tutoring allow students to interact with tutors in real time, through the Internet. Tutoring is therefore delivered at the teachable moment, when students have an immediate need for instruction. Educators must therefore inform parents, caregivers, and students that online tutoring is available. These individuals may not know that help is available online.

Parents and caregivers can contact an institution by e-mail to set up a session for their children. It is also possible to get customer service help from real-time chats. Once students are registered and want help with schoolwork (homework), all they need to do is upload the assignment to the website. The company provides a quote for the service, if it is not a free service provider. Online companies that charge for services vary in terms of cost and method of payment. Credit cards are generally accepted by most online providers. Some companies offer other payment alternatives, such as checks or payment through PayPal. Many online tutoring companies also offer a free trial.

Online tutoring helps students succeed academically, boosts retention, and improves learning. The online tutoring provided by many institutions fills a niche that cannot be filled in today's schools alone. To deliver lasting success for students in school and beyond, though, online tutoring programs need to address the components of successful tutoring programs discussed in chapter 3, likewise revealed by other international tutoring programs.

Chapter Five

Student Motivation and Parental Involvement in Tutoring

This chapter looks at student motivation and the importance of motivational factors in tutoring. In addition, it focuses on the significance as well as the best practices for parental involvement. The chapter also highlights the National Parent Association and Family Engagement in Education Act and ends with final thoughts on tutoring.

MOTIVATION

Motivation deals with a student's desire to participate in the learning process. Brophy (1998; 2004) defines motivation as a theoretical construct used to explain the initiation, direction, intensity, and persistence of behavior, especially goal-directed behavior. Meece and McColskey (2001) indicate that motivation is a personal trait that depends on the genetic nature and the childhood experiences of a student. Pintrich and Schunk (2002) view motivation as the primary contributing factor of a student's learning and success in school. Motivation is the drive behind all the engagements of an individual.

Many researchers believe that tutoring can foster motivation and that successful tutoring is often linked to motivational factors. Research reveals that motivation directly influences how often students use learning strategies, how well they perform on curriculum-related tests, how much they persevere and maintain skills after tutoring ends. The Common Core State Standards list motivation in the Model of Text Complexity as an example of reader and task considerations, which focus on the variables specific to the individual reader. The standards stress that highly motivated readers are often willing to put in the extra effort required to read harder texts.

In the book *The Death and Life of the Great American School System*, Diane Ravitch (2010) indicates that the No Child Left Behind Act neglects to acknowledge that students share in the responsibility for their academic performance. Ravitch believes that students are not just passive recipients of their teachers' influence. She indicates that nowhere in the federal accountability scheme were there measures of indicators of students' diligence, effort, and motivation. Ravitch questions whether students attend school regularly or do their homework or pay attention in class, or if students are motivated to succeed. Ravitch insists that the answers to these questions affect a student's school performance as much as or more than their teachers' skill.

A strategy recommended to motivate students in tutoring is goal setting (Rubin, 1997 and Swanson & Hertz, 1998). Goal setting directs students to focus their attention, motivates them to persist in meeting the objectives, and helps them formulate strategies to accomplish a goal (Locke et al., 1981). Goals must be specific and provide somewhat of a challenge for the student. It is also important that students not become disheartened or exhausted attempting to achieve an unattainable goal (Swanson & Hertz, 1998).

Students should receive sufficient opportunities to set their own goals in tutoring and make a commitment to achieve them. The development and monitoring of goals must, however, include the student's tutor. Swanson and Hertz believe that the confidence of students is enhanced as they become more responsible for their learning and are more motivated as learners. The praise and recognition that tutors provide students also motivate them to achieve higher levels of success, which can drive students' motivation and allow them to build confidence.

Personal communication with Morency (2014), an educator and a private tutor who has tutored students for more than a decade, indicates that student's motivation and parental involvement are priceless for a student's academic success. Morency works with students of all ages and backgrounds, from pre-kindergarten through college level. She attests that skilled tutors acknowledge that each student learns differently. Each student, Morency says, brings to the tutoring experience a different amount of knowledge and a different approach toward learning.

Morency agrees that it is the tutor's responsibility to help build the confidence level of his or her student during tutoring. She states that students who set goals are more likely to strive toward the accomplishment of the stated goals. Morency affirms that some students need the one-on-one attention that tutoring provides to achieve success in school, to allow them to perform at or above grade level.

THE IMPORTANCE OF MOTIVATIONAL FACTORS

Tutors must take into account the motivational and affective side of tutoring (Harris, 1980). Tutoring research suggests that successful tutoring supports students' academic achievement and their motivation toward the subject matter. As a result, effective tutors are cognizant of the effect of motivational and cognitive factors when working with students.

Mark Lepper and Ruth Chabay (1988) indicate that motivational factors act as a critical cognitive factor to determine the results of tutoring relations. A survey of tutored students suggests that students expected their tutors to give them the assistance they need academically, as well as provide affective support (Krabbe & Krabbe, 1995). These researchers indicate that students list fondness for their tutor's personality more often than their tutor's skill in teaching the material.

Motivational considerations guide tutors' selection of topics and the ways in which they provide feedback (Lepper et al. 1997). In an observational study of highly effective tutors, Lepper et al. created the acronym INSPIRE, in which tutors were listed as follows:

- Intelligent—knows the subject matter well and recognizes the difficulty level of problems and concepts
- Nurturant—establishes and maintains personal rapport and empathy with students
- Socratic—provides almost no facts, solutions, or explanations, but elicits these from students by questioning
- Progressive—begins work with students at a level of difficulty where the students are comfortable and then challenges students by gradually increasing the difficulty of the material discussed

- Indirect—conveys expectations in a polite and discreet manner and provides both negative and positive feedback by implication
- Reflective—asks students to reflect on their progress by asking them to explain, summarize, or write down what they have learned, therefore strengthening their new knowledge and skills
- Encouraging—uses strategies to motivate students and boost their confidence

The model for tutoring success based on the acronym INSPIRE describes the characteristics of highly effective tutors. These tutors focus on the cognitive development of students and their affective and motivational needs.

Table 5.1 shows the characteristics and examples of behaviors from INSPIRE: A Model for Tutoring Success.

Motivation can be a challenge for some students, but students who have a strong aspiration to gain knowledge are more likely to succeed academically. According to Sweet and Guthrie (1996), students who are intrinsically motivated sustain lifelong literacy. Intrinsic motivators are aims that develop within a learner that result from their personal interests and private experiences.

Ravitch (2010) believes that parents are primarily responsible for their children's behavior and attitudes, and therefore, with their child's educators, can academically engage children on a regular basis to achieve academic success. Motivation is important because it affects students' lives every day. Most important, all behaviors, actions, thoughts, and beliefs are influenced by one's inner drive to succeed.

Table 5.1. INSPIRE: A Model for Tutoring Success. INSPIRE = Intelligent, Nurturant, Socratic, Progressive, Indirect, Reflective, Encouraging.

INSPIRE Characteristics	Examples of behaviors
1. Intelligent	
Strong subject-matter knowledge	• Provide relevant historical information (instructive or motivational). • Use concrete manipulatives and visual models for illustrating difficult concepts. • Produce a wide variety of real-world analogies.
Strong subject-specific pedagogical knowledge	• Know which problems will be difficult. • Know what types of errors are most likely. • Know which problems appear to be more (or less) difficult to students than they really are.
General pedagogical knowledge	Use and articulate instructional and motivational techniques identified in the rest of this table.
2. Nurturant	
Highly supportive of students	• Establish personal rapport early. • Empathize with students' difficulties. • Show confidence in students' ability to succeed.
3. Socratic, not didactic	
Questions, not directions	• More than 90 percent of remarks are in the form of questions. • Questions are often leading or informative. • Draw as much as possible from the student and impose as little as necessary.
Hints, not answers	• Offer hints or suggestions and avoid directly giving answers. • Act to help students take the next step on their own. • Persist with many sequential hints, starting with general ones, and becoming more specific as necessary.

Productive versus nonproductive errors	• Sophisticated understanding of different types of errors, and how to respond effectively to them. • Ignore small errors when they do not prevent arrival at a correct answer (although these may lead to subsequent problems to target difficulties). • Able to identify "productive errors" which can be used to guide students towards discovery of misconceptions. • Some are deliberately allowed to occur so that they can be systematically "debugged." • Able to detect and act upon "nonproductive errors," which may lead students astray, and which need more explicit intervention.
4. Progressive	
Problem progression	• Systematic progression, starting with problems that diagnose students' initial levels of knowledge and misunderstanding. • Subsequent problems selected for the correction of misunderstandings before moving on to further challenges.
Systematic debugging of student errors	• Goal is to prompt students to discover for themselves the reasons for their errors. • Routinely begin with general hints and questions, progressing to more specific questioning types of help only as needed.
Progressive routines	Effectively structure tutoring sessions using recurring routines, helping focus students' attention on appropriate issues at different phases of the tutorial.
5. Indirect	
Negative feedback	• Avoid overt criticism by posing questions that indirectly imply the existence of an error and, sometimes, the location of that error. • Goal is to prompt students into retracing their own steps and "catching" their own errors.

Positive feedback	Less likely to provide explicit praise to students, especially praise directed at the person rather than the process of problem solving.
6. Reflective Articulation	Have students reflect aloud immediately after a successful problem solution. This (i) helps gain information from students about possible misunderstandings, and (ii) helps students to understand at a conceptual level. (Example: Have student keep a written list in their own words of general "lessons" they have learned.)
Explanation	Periodically ask students to explain answers and procedures. If incomplete, elaborate on the student's response, thus modeling a more complete explanation.
Generalization	Periodically ask students to relate work to other types of problems or to real-world situation that they are familiar with and interested in.
7. Encouraging Confidence	Concerned with bolstering students' feelings of competence and mastery. (Example: Emphasize the difficulty of the problems, (i) implicitly giving students an excuse if they do have difficulty and (ii) increasing the value of success.)
Challenge	• Likely to challenge students—goad them into a desire to "show" the tutor just how much they can accomplish. • Able to present problems that will be challenging, though not impossible.
Curiosity	• Try to pique students' curiosity so they want to find answers on their own. • Ask students to predict similarities or differences between current and previous problems. • Deliberately highlight inconsistencies to provoke students into seeking some resolution.

Control	• Offer students choices.
• Comply with their requests.
• Emphasize a student's sense of agency directly.
• Avoid direct didactic methods that could undermine a learner's sense of control.
Contextualization	• Place abstract problems into meaningful and interesting contexts.
• Personalize problems so relevance can be seen in familiar real-world contexts that students care about.
• Use of enjoyable and provocative stories improves motivation.

Source: Lepper, M. R., & M. Woolverton (2002). *Improving academic achievement: Impact of psychological factors in education.* Chapter 7: The wisdom of practice: Lessons learned from the study of highly effective tutors. Edited by Aronson, J. Emerald Group Publishing. Retrieved from http://www.eos.ubc.ca/research/cwsei/resources/INSPIRE-Guidelines.pdf.

This model for tutoring success is due to: Lepper, M. R., M. F. Drake, & T. O'Donnell-Johnson (1997). *Scaffolding techniques of expert human tutors.* In K. Hogan & M. Pressley (eds.), Scaffolding student learning: Instructional approaches and issues (pp. 108–144). Cambridge: Brookline. Retrieved from ERIC database (ED422375), http://eric.ed.gov/.

PARENTAL INVOLVEMENT

Parent involvement positively affects student success in school and plays a vital role to support learning. Coleman et al. (1966), in a well-known view from the report "Equality of Educational Opportunity," (commonly known as the Coleman Report), found that families made the difference, not schools. It was found that the main determinant of United States students' achievement was their family background. The finding has since been confirmed in many studies in other countries and resulted in considerable attention being given to parental involvement in education.

The definition of parental involvement is the participation of parents in regular, two-way and meaningful communication, which involves student academic learning and other school activities (U.S. Department of Education, 2004). It also takes into account that parents should play an integral role to assist their child's learning, being actively involved in their child's education at school and full partners in their child's education. Parents should be included in decision making and on advisory committees, to help in the schooling of their children.

The words *parent/s* or *family/ies* are being used to include both single and multiple parents, stepparents, legal guardians, and any other caregivers who play a significant role in a student's life. Likewise the term *educator/s* is being used to include tutor/s.

SIGNIFICANCE OF PARENTAL INVOLVEMENT

Decades of research provides evidence that parents play a critical role in helping their children prepare for school and lifelong academic success. Parents are essentially a child's first and most important educators. The earlier in a child's educational process that parents become involved, the more valuable the achievement effects. Continued parental involvement is essential through students' school years, though.

Beth Sattes (1985) indicates that the beneficial effect of parent involvement on student achievement includes improved attendance, motivation, and behavior. In 1987 Henderson reviewed forty-nine studies of parent involvement in children's learning at home, instructional programs at school, and support of their children's school. She concludes that all forms of parental involvement have positive effects on student achievement. Shaver and Walls (1998) and Jordan et al.

(2000) also confirm that there is a direct positive relationship between parental involvement and students' academic achievement.

In 2002, Anne Henderson and Karen Mapp conducted a comprehensive study on parent involvement that comprised more than fifty-one research studies. These researchers found that students with involved parents, no matter what their income or background, were more likely to earn higher grades and test scores and enroll in higher-level programs; be promoted, pass their classes, and earn credits; attend school regularly; have better social skills, show improved behavior, and adapt well to school; and graduate and go on to postsecondary education.

The U.S. Department of Education (2004), also confirmed that students with involved parents are more likely to earn higher grades, attend school regularly, and pursue postsecondary education, regardless of their socioeconomic status. Flouri and Buchanan (2004) and Bonci et al. (2010) make known that parents' high expectations and taking part in learning activities overcome the potential negative achievement influences of other background factors such as family size, parents' educational level, and socioeconomic status. Researchers Xu et al. (2010) indicate that educational achievement is greatly influenced by parents' high expectations.

Children with supportive home learning environments show increased literacy development, better peer interactions, fewer behavior problems, and more motivation and persistence during learning activities (Fantuzzo et al., 2004). Longitudinal studies of low-income children show that high parental involvement offsets the risks of children growing up in households where their parents have low levels of schooling (Dearing et al., 2006).

Overall, parent involvement in student's learning has been shown in numerous research studies to be positively related to achievement. Parental involvement even involves parents finding outside assistance, such as tutoring for their children, to receive academic support to enhance their achievement. Regardless of the types of parental involvement and extent of the involvement, different types of parental involvement have a positive effect on students' academic success.

Parental involvement is particularly significant in the primary grades. When students are in the primary grades, parents usually feel less defensive toward their schooling. Parents are also more enthusiastic to work with their children and educators in the early years. The successes of parental involvement in other grades are highly reliant on parental support in the primary grades. Educators at school or in a tutoring program outside of school who encourage parental involvement early in a child's education have a more lasting effect on students' learning outcomes.

Everyone benefits when parents, schools, and communities collaborate to improve student learning. William Jeynes's (2005) meta-analysis research indicates that the benefits to parents are that they face more confidence in the schools; teachers have higher opinions of parents and higher expectations for their children. Besides, parents have greater confidence in themselves and their ability to help their children learn at home, and there is a greater likelihood that parents will enroll in continuing education to advance their own schooling. The benefits for the schools and communities are improved teacher morale, higher ratings of teachers by parents, more support from families, higher student achievement, and better standings in the community.

Many educators agree that the lack of parental involvement has negative effects on students' academic performances. Conversely, parental involvement shows a consistent, positive relationship in students' achievement and growth.

BEST PRACTICES FOR PARENTAL INVOLVEMENT

The Ohio Department of Education (2013) listed the following best practices for parental involvement, based on the State Board of Education's Parent and Family Involvement Policy (2007), Parent Teacher Association National Standards for Family-School Partnerships (2009), and Epstein et al. (2009) framework of six types of parent involvement:

- Create a welcoming school climate.
- Provide families with information related to child development and create supportive learning environments.
- Establish effective school-to-home and home-to-school communication.
- Strengthen families' knowledge and skills to support and extend their children's learning at home and in the community.
- Engage families in school planning, leadership, and meaningful volunteer opportunities.
- Connect students and families to community resources that strengthen and support students' learning and well-being.

All parents, regardless of ethnicity, educational background, gender, disability, or socioeconomic status, want their children to do well in school and life. Many parents will partner with institutions of learning that will help their children achieve success. Educators must build collaborative and trusting relationships with all parents and inform them of ways they too can help.

NATIONAL PARENT TEACHER ASSOCIATION AND FAMILY ENGAGEMENT IN EDUCATION ACT

In 2014 the National Parent Teacher Association (PTA) teamed up with Sylvan to offer free and discounted educational resources to parents and students. The PTA is one of the largest volunteer child advocacy associations in the nation and is comprised of families, students, administrators, and community leaders. These individuals are dedicated to the educational success of children and the promotion of parental involvement in schools.

Sylvan, located in North America, is a leading provider of tutoring for students of all ages, grades, and skill levels. Sylvan has trained and certified educators that provide personal tutoring programs in reading, writing, mathematics, study skills, and test-prep for college entrance and state exams.

The association between the PTA and Sylvan allows PTA members access to education experts, resources, and services to help children succeed. Sylvan offers its PTA-member students access to a Sylvan Insight Assessment. The assessment identifies students' academic strengths and weaknesses, as well as their attitudes about school and learning. The assessment offer at a discounted price is designed to help families and educators determine the right support a child needs to excel.

Since the passage of the Elementary and Secondary Education Act (ESEA) in 1965, parent involvement later extended to include families, has been a key component of social justice, equity, and a high-quality education (Redding et al., 2004). Today the term parent involvement is sometimes interchanged with family engagement. Family engagement recognizes that grandparents and other family members can play a significant role in a student's life. The term family engagement indicates a shared and continuous responsibility for student achievement and learning across multiple settings. Family engagement also suggests a deeper level of commitment and participation than involvement.

In 2013 the Family Engagement in Education Act was introduced to establish a critical effort to provide comprehensive reauthorization of the ESEA/No Child Left Behind Act. The act amends Title I—Improving the Academic Achievement of the Disadvantaged of the ESEA. The act seeks to target capacity-building and technical assistance for effective family engagement strategies. It also encourages state and school district flexibility to identify programs that work best for specific communities.

The Family Engagement in Education Act allows states to reserve school improvement funds to do the following:

a. Award a grant to a statewide nonprofit organization to establish a Statewide Family Engagement Center. The center provides comprehensive training, technical assistance, and capacity-building to local educational agencies (LEAs), organizations that support family-school partnerships, and other organizations that carry out parent education and family engagement in education programs.
b. Award grants to nonprofit organizations, Indian tribes, or organizations that partner with LEAs or schools to establish and operate Local Family Engagement Centers. These centers assist families in becoming engaged in their children's education.
c. Develop and implement a statewide family engagement in education plan.

The Family Engagement in Education Act is endorsed by the following organizations:

- National PTA
- American School Counselor Association
- Campaign for Youth Justice
- National Association of Elementary School Principals
- National Association of Secondary School Principals
- National Center for Family Literacy
- National Family, School, and Community Engagement Working Group
- National Indian Education Association
- Parents as Teachers
- School Social Work Association of America
- TESOL (Teachers of English to Speakers of Other Languages) International Association
- United Way Worldwide
- PTAs in the states of Alabama, Alaska, Arkansas, Arizona, California, Colorado, Delaware, District of Columbia, Florida, Georgia, Idaho, Illinois, Iowa, Kansas, Kentucky, Louisiana, Maine, Maryland, Massachusetts, Michigan, Minnesota, Missouri, Mississippi, Montana, Nebraska, Nevada, New Hampshire, New Jersey, New Mexico, New York, North Carolina, North Dakota, Oklahoma, Ohio, Oregon, Pennsylvania, Rhode Island, South Carolina, South Dakota, Tennessee, Texas, Utah, Vermont, Virginia, Wisconsin, Washington, West Virginia, and Wyoming
- PTSA (Parents, Teachers, and Students Association) in the states of Connecticut, Hawaii, and Michigan
- Europe PTA

Family engagement is rapidly shifting from a low-priority recommendation to an integral part of education reform efforts (Mapp & Kuttner, 2013).

The findings on family engagement from Congress are as follows:

1. Family engagement in a child's education raises student achievement, improves behavior and attendance, decreases drop-out rates, and improves the emotional and physical well-being of children.
2. Families are critical determinants of children's school readiness, as well as of students' decision to pursue higher education.
3. Effective family engagement is a great equalizer for students and contributes to their increased academic achievement, regardless of their parents' education level, ethnicity, or socioeconomic background.
4. Research on school improvement identifies meaningful partnerships with families and communities as a critical requirement needed to turn around chronically low-performing schools.
5. Positive benefits for children, youth, families, and schools are maximized through effective family engagement as a shared responsibility. In such an arrangement, schools and other community agencies and organizations are committed to reaching out to engage families in meaningful ways, and families are committed to actively support their children's learning and development. The arrangement is continuous through a child's life from birth to young adulthood and reinforces learning that takes place in all settings.

The U.S. Department in 2007 indicated that other organizations, such as the Parental Information and Resource Centers, were regarded by Congress under the ESEA to provide parents, schools, and other organizations working with families with the information and support needed to understand how children develop and what they need to succeed in school. See appendix C.

A partnership needs to exist between parents and educators who are the main influencers in students' academic lives. Educators need to communicate regularly, clearly, and openly with parents about the status of their children's progress and the nature of the work being done. In addition, educators should provide suggestions to parents that they too can implement to help their children. Parental involvement/family engagement is more effective when there is shared respect between the parents/families and their child's educators. Children who have parents involved in their schooling also are likely to become parents that do the same thing.

Research repeatedly reveals that parent involvement/family engagement in a child's education not only increases student achievement, it improves attendance and reduces dropout rates. Further, parents are empowered, teachers have better assurance, and students do better in school and beyond, resulting in improved schools and stronger communities.

Communication is the foundation of effective partnerships. The communication between home and school should be consistent, collaborative, and noteworthy (Lockett, 1999). Individuals who communicate effectively develop positive relationships and make great progress. Effective tutors listen and communicate and collaborate early and often with parents, and at times, the students' educators. The teaching and learning of students is enriched by the involvement/engagement of parents in their children's education.

See appendix C for a list of resources for engaging parents in education (U.S. Department of Education, 2007).

FINAL THOUGHTS

Education is an integral part of our society and a pathway to opportunity and a better life. Tutoring is the oldest form of education and remains a popular form of instruction that has been documented extensively worldwide. Tutoring allows no child to be left behind, and when well-planned and implemented, strengthens teaching and learning to improve students' success in school. Tutoring is no longer associated primarily with poor academic skills or a need for remediation. Tutoring is an instructional method that can benefit any student at some point in their schooling, whether online, face-to-face, or by some other format.

Tutoring is a component of many educational programs and an effective teaching method supported by contemporary research. In 1984 Benjamin Bloom, a distinguished American educational psychologist, reviewed research that measured the effects of one-on-one tutoring and discovered that tutored students achieved academic results two standard deviations over those who were not tutored. Bloom's research was famously referred to as "The 2 Sigma Problem," and tutoring was noted twice as effective as conventional instruction.

In 1982, Cohen et al. supported Bloom's findings of the effectiveness of tutoring in a comparative meta-analysis of sixty-five studies of tutoring in various subject areas. In 86 percent of the studies, tutored students achieved higher scores than those in a control group. Gordon et al. (2007), in the ground-breaking book *The Tutoring Revolution: Applying Research for Best Practices, Policy Implications, and Student Achievement*, consider tutoring an integral component for education reform.

In a meta-analysis of more than eighty-six tutoring programs, Ritter et al. (2009) found that overall volunteer tutoring had a positive effect on student achievement, compared to students who were not tutored. Reinheimer and McKenzie (2011), in a causal-comparative study of students with undeclared majors, reported that tutoring college students increases retention of underprepared students and students at risk for failure.

The improvement of students at risk for education failure is a major concern for government, schools, and communities. A great deal of evidence consistent over decades reveals that numerous students across the United States are not performing well in school. Students that do not develop the necessary academic skills are at risk for continued school failure, underemployment, and the inability to contribute completely in society. Well-planned and implemented tutoring programs could definitely improve the academic performance of America's students.

Private tutoring is a growth industry, and in the United States, four to six billion dollars a year is spent on tutoring children. In 2014, the market research firm Global Industry Analysts (GIA) released a study that states that the global private tutoring market is projected to surpass $102.8 billion by 2018. According to GIA, the rapidly increasing private tutoring market is being driven by the failure of the standard education systems to satisfy the unique needs of students, combined with growing parental desire to secure the best possible education for their children in a highly competitive global economy.

The need for tutors today is greater than ever, and parents need to be provided with appropriate information that is based on theory and research that they can use to help their children achieve academic success. Educators must therefore be concerned with theories and principles of human learning, teaching, and instruction, all within the framework of theory-derived educational materials, programs, strategies, and techniques that enhance lifelong educational undertakings and approaches.

The theories of learning offer stakeholders a deeper appreciation and understanding of learning. The theories are from educational experts that inform stakeholders, and stakeholders in return can use these theories to benefit students' learning within tutoring programs. The theories are categorized under three main categories or philosophical frameworks: behaviorism, cognitivism, and constructivism.

Behaviorism focuses on the objectively observable aspects of learning. Cognitive theories look further than behavior to explain brain-based learning. Constructivism views learning as a process in which the learner actively constructs or builds new ideas or concepts. Research reveals that tutoring empowers students to develop cognitive skills that enable them to understand and express complex ideas. Principles of learning drawn from both cognitive and constructivist thinking offer the strongest contemporary tutoring methods (Gordon, 2008).

Tutoring programs can benefit from the selection of one or several tutoring formats, such as one-on-one, home-based, peer, cross-age, small-group, online, volunteer, after-school, and sometimes during-school programs. Regardless of the tutoring format, tutoring helps solidify what students have learned or are struggling with in the classroom.

Today, with our nation's increased attention on the achievements of students in school, it is important for learning institutions, whether schools, tutoring establishments, or individual tutors, to show the value of what is being undertaken and its program impact. Evaluations and research-based practices exemplify the values of continuous quality improvement that can be achieved in any tutoring program.

Evaluations are proven to be useful tools that determine improvement toward or accomplishments of the objectives specified by any program. An evaluation's main purpose is to provide information for decision making and improve the quality of a program by identifying program strengths and weaknesses. The findings allow organizations to promote learning and improve organizational effectiveness. In a tutoring program, evaluations can help stakeholders focus resources on the elements of a program most beneficial to the students and tutors.

Partnership and communication among participants in tutoring programs is key to success. A student's success depends upon the relations among many individuals, including the involvement of students, educators, parents, public officials, local organizations, and the larger community. Tutors need to continue to play a major role in connecting classrooms, homes, and schools.

Tutoring offers a certain degree of freedom from classroom constraints. Many researchers have identified effective components of successful tutoring programs that improve the chances for a positive impact on student achievement. These researchers reveal that successful tutoring programs must be intensive, consistent, and structured; use diagnostic/development; have intensive and ongoing training and feedback for tutors; have systematic reflective assessments by tutors of student progress; and provide close coordination with teacher and classroom. Successful tutoring programs must be planned, implemented, monitored, and modified systematically.

Online tutoring and homework assistance programs offer schools an effective way to provide key academic support to students. These programs have become more real-world, because of the continual advancement of technology and globalization. Some online tutoring programs allow students with learning disabilities and other disadvantages to get custom-designed tutoring assignments to achieve their learning goals. Technology and online tutoring/homework assistance programs allow students to interact with tutors in real time, through the Internet. Tutoring is therefore delivered at the teachable moment, when students have an immediate need for instruction.

For children to reach their full academic potential, however, a rapport between parents and tutors or parents and the school system must be developed as soon as a student enters an institution of learning. In a study by Thomas Koerner (1991) several nationally honored principals in the United States believed that although principals would continue to be decision makers and organizers, they must also be bridge builders among local groups and involve parents and teachers in decisions that affect students.

According to the U.S. Department of Education (2004), parental involvement is the participation of parents in regular, two-way, and meaningful communication, which involves student academic learning and other school activities. Parental involvement is highly important for pushing institutions of learning to higher standards and engaging parents in an active role in the school curriculum (Machen et al., 2005).

Today the term parent involvement is sometimes interchanged with family engagement. It recognizes that grandparents and other family members can play an important role in a student's life. The term family engagement indicates a shared and continuous responsibility for student achievement and learning across multiple settings. Family engagement also suggests a deeper level of commitment and participation than involvement.

On July 11, 2013, the Family Engagement in Education Act of 2013 was introduced. The act provides school districts the flexibility to identify programming that works best for individual communities and resources to build effective family engagement strategies. On July 31, 2014, the White House in collaboration with the W. K. Kellogg Foundation and other partners, hosted an event to expand the national conversation on the profound influence that transformative family engagement practices have on children's school readiness and overall success.

On the whole, parental involvement/family engagement is essential to students' academic success. Students strive harder and perform better when parents/families are actively engaged in their education and consequently this involvement/engagement is encouraged at all grade levels.

Educators need to gain the support of parents and launch the effort to obtain funding for programs such as tutoring, to afford every student an opportunity to obtain learning support if needed. Furthermore, educators need to inform parents of outside sources that are available that can help their children with their learning needs. In 2008, Bridgeland et al. indicate that there is a gap between the number of students who desired tutoring and the number of students who gained access to it. Consequently, it appears that many more students could benefit from well-planned tutoring programs.

Tutoring, when combined with other forms of personalized instruction, can be effective with even struggling students or students with disabilities. It provides some disabled students the chance to contribute to the overall general education instruction in their classroom. Students that experience difficulty attaining the academic and social competencies required for successful involvement in school and society face the possibility of being undereducated, underemployed, and underprepared to participate successfully in life in their later years. With the support of a tutor, or by having a child involved in an effective tutoring program, the chances of a student's success far offset the prospects of failure.

Educational researchers and psychologists, among others, have found that tutoring is one of the most effective ways to increase student performance across disciplines, improving grades, persistence in class, and retention. Tutoring, a privilege once afforded only to the children of the wealthy, is now commonly accessible through schools, colleges, universities, libraries, churches, community agencies, and public and private tutoring institutions, allowing all students the potential to achieve academic success in school.

Tutoring must play a significant role in our nation's initiative to improve learning for all students. Well-planned and implemented tutoring programs in schools, private, or nonprofit institutions can yield significant gains in academic achievement for every student. Tutoring reinforces what is taught in the classroom and amplifies students' learning. It allows them to transfer knowledge back to the classroom or retain the information and transfer or apply it in other contexts, so that students become independent, successful learners.

Appendices

APPENDIX A

Joint Committee on Standards for Educational Evaluation: Program Evaluation Standards Statements

Source: Yarbrough, D. B., L. M. Shulha, R. K. Hopson, & F. A. Caruthers (2011). *The program evaluation standards: A guide for evaluators and evaluation users.* 3rd ed. Thousand Oaks, CA: Sage.

The intent of the standards is to ensure useful, feasible, ethical, and sound evaluation of education programs, projects, and materials. These standards were sponsored by professional organizations such as those mentioned in chapter 3. The following presents a summary of the standards; however, further information and explanation can be obtained from *The Program Evaluation Standards: A Guide for Evaluators and Evaluation Users*, Third Edition, available at http://www.sagepub.com/booksProdDesc.nav?prodId=Book230597&_requestid=255617.

UTILITY (U) STANDARDS

The utility standards are intended to increase the extent to which program stakeholders find evaluation processes and products valuable in meeting their needs.

- U1 Evaluator Credibility. Evaluations should be conducted by qualified people who establish and maintain credibility in the evaluation context.
- U2 Attention to Stakeholders. Evaluations should devote attention to the full range of individuals and groups invested in the program and affected by its evaluation.
- U3 Negotiated Purposes. Evaluation purposes should be identified and continually negotiated based on the needs of stakeholders.
- U4 Explicit Values. Evaluations should clarify and specify the individual and cultural values underpinning purposes, processes, and judgments.
- U5 Relevant Information. Evaluation information should serve the identified and emergent needs of stakeholders.
- U6 Meaningful Processes and Products. Evaluations should construct activities, descriptions, and judgments in ways that encourage participants to rediscover, reinterpret, or revise their understandings and behaviors.
- U7 Timely and Appropriate Communicating and Reporting. Evaluations should attend to the continuing information needs of their multiple audiences.
- U8 Concern for Consequences and Influence. Evaluations should promote responsible and adaptive use while guarding against unintended negative consequences and misuse.

FEASIBILITY (F) STANDARDS

The feasibility standards are intended to increase evaluation effectiveness and efficiency.

- F1 Project Management. Evaluations should use effective project management strategies.
- F2 Practical Procedures. Evaluation procedures should be practical and responsive to the way the program operates.
- F3 Contextual Viability. Evaluations should recognize, monitor, and balance the cultural and political interests and needs of individuals and groups.
- F4 Resource Use. Evaluations should use resources effectively and efficiently.

PROPRIETY (P) STANDARDS

The propriety standards support what is proper, fair, legal, right, and just in evaluations.

- P1 Responsive and Inclusive Orientation. Evaluations should be responsive to stakeholders and their communities.
- P2 Formal Agreements. Evaluation agreements should be negotiated to make obligations explicit and take into account the needs, expectations, and cultural contexts of clients and other stakeholders.
- P3 Human Rights and Respect. Evaluations should be designed and conducted to protect human and legal rights and maintain the dignity of participants and other stakeholders.
- P4 Clarity and Fairness. Evaluations should be understandable and fair in addressing stakeholder needs and purposes.

- P5 Transparency and Disclosure. Evaluations should provide complete descriptions of findings, limitations, and conclusions to all stakeholders, unless doing so would violate legal and propriety obligations.
- P6 Conflicts of Interests. Evaluations should openly and honestly identify and address real or perceived conflicts of interests that may compromise the evaluation.
- P7 Fiscal Responsibility. Evaluations should account for all expended resources and comply with sound fiscal procedures and processes.

ACCURACY (A) STANDARDS

The accuracy standards are intended to increase the dependability and truthfulness of evaluation representations, propositions, and findings, especially those that support interpretations and judgments about quality.

- A1 Justified Conclusions and Decisions. Evaluation conclusions and decisions should be explicitly justified in the cultures and contexts where they have consequences.
- A2 Valid Information. Evaluation information should serve the intended purposes and support valid interpretations.
- A3 Reliable Information. Evaluation procedures should yield sufficiently dependable and consistent information for the intended uses.
- A4 Explicit Program and Context Descriptions. Evaluations should document programs and their contexts with appropriate detail and scope for the evaluation purposes.

- A5 Information Management. Evaluations should employ systematic information collection, review, verification, and storage methods.
- A6 Sound Designs and Analyses. Evaluations should employ technically adequate designs and analyses that are appropriate for evaluation purposes.
- A7 Explicit Evaluation Reasoning. Evaluation reasoning leading from information and analyses to findings, interpretations, conclusions, and judgments should be clearly and completely documented.
- A8 Communication and Reporting. Evaluation communications should have adequate scope and guard against misconceptions, biases, distortions, and errors.

EVALUATION (E) ACCOUNTABILITY STANDARDS

The evaluation accountability standards encourage adequate documentation of evaluations and a meta-evaluative perspective focused on improvement and accountability for evaluation processes and products.

- E1 Evaluation Documentation. Evaluations should fully document their negotiated purposes and implemented designs, procedures, data, and outcomes.
- E2 Internal Meta-evaluation. Evaluators should use these and other applicable standards to examine the accountability of the evaluation design, procedures employed, information collected, and outcomes.
- E3 External Meta-evaluation. Program evaluation sponsors, clients, evaluators, and other stakeholders should encourage the

conduct of external meta-evaluations using these and other applicable standards.

APPENDIX B

The Saint Paul Public Schools Best Practices for Tutoring Programs

Source: Saint Paul Public Schools Foundation (2013). *Best practices for tutoring programs: A guide to quality.* 2nd ed. Saint Paul, MN: Greater Twin Cities United Way. Used with permission from the Saint Paul Public Schools Foundation.

The Saint Paul Public Schools are grounded in best practices for tutoring programs. Each of the eight practices are research based and proven to achieve positive outcomes for students. The *Saint Paul Public Schools Best Practices for Tutoring Programs: A Guide to Quality* is a research-based guide for implementing and sustaining effective tutoring programs. Tutoring programs in any setting and at any level of development can use the guide to improve their program quality and increase achievement for the students they serve.

The Saint Paul Public Schools' eight best practices for tutoring programs are as follows:

Best Practice	Best-Practice Standard	Indicators of Best Practice
1. Organizational Management	A best-practice tutoring program has clear organizational structure and management that supports student success.	• Tutoring program mission statement clearly communicates what the program aspires to accomplish. • Tutoring program is aligned with the supporting organization's mission. • Programmatic activities are aligned with the organization's strategic plan.

		• Tutoring program has a yearly project-specific work plan that accurately reflects program goals, activities, and responsibilities. • The organization provides staff with opportunities for professional and skill development as well as performance appraisals. • The organization supports the development of management skills for program leadership.
2. Cultural Proficiency	A best-practice tutoring program demonstrates cultural competence and strives for cultural proficiency.	• Tutoring program prioritizes cultural proficiency to meet the diverse needs of all students. • Tutoring program prioritizes selecting staff and tutors who are culturally competent. • Tutoring program provides initial cultural competency training. • Tutoring program provides ongoing training to support cultural proficiency.
3. Student Recruitment and Management	A best-practice tutoring program implements a clear plan to recruit and manage student participants.	• Tutoring program has a clearly defined target group. • Tutoring program implements a plan to recruit student participants. • Tutoring program has a standard process for enrolling or registering new students.

		• Tutoring program promotes high student attendance and participation throughout the year. • Tutoring program has a student retention plan, including specific goals for participation in tutoring program from year to year.
4. Tutor Recruitment and Management	A best-practice tutoring program follows a clear plan to recruit and manage tutors.	• Tutoring program implements a tutor recruitment plan. • Tutoring program establishes a tutor screening policy that includes background and reference checks. • Tutoring program selects tutors who are appropriate for the student target groups. • Tutoring program has a designated staff member who provides support, guidance, and feedback to tutors. • Tutoring program has a tutor retention plan, including specific goals for long-term involvement. • The program holds tutor appreciation or recognition events.
5. Tutor Training	A best-practice tutoring program provides initial and ongoing training opportunities to build the capacity of tutors to best meet student needs.	• Tutoring program prioritizes tutor training by implementing a comprehensive training plan. • Tutoring program requires an initial program orientation for every tutor. • Tutoring program requires initial training for every tutor.

		• Tutoring program provides ongoing training and professional development opportunities for tutors.
6. Tutoring Intervention	A best practice tutoring program provides high-quality tutoring interventions of sufficient duration and frequency that are aligned with classroom instruction.	• Student participants attend tutoring frequently and consistently with a minimum of 90 minutes per week. • Tutoring interventions are tailored to individual student needs and progress. • Tutoring program provides a lesson plan or outline for each tutoring session. • Tutoring interventions are aligned with school district curriculum. • Tutoring program implements low student-tutor ratios to foster positive relationships.
7. Engagement with Families, Schools, and Communities	A best-practice tutoring program recognizes and engages families, schools, and communities as necessary partners for improving student achievement.	• Tutoring program is committed to partnering with families, schools, and community. • Tutoring program communicates with and engages regularly with families. • Tutoring program communicates with and engages regularly with schools. • Tutoring program communicates with and engages regularly with community partners.
8. Evaluation	A best-practice tutoring program uses systematic evaluation to	• Tutoring program promotes a culture of evaluation.

assess its impact on student outcomes and ensure continuous improvement.	• Tutoring program uses evaluation results to continually improve the quality and effectiveness of its tutoring. • Tutoring program has a logic model that aligns program activities with expected outcomes. • Tutoring program uses an evaluation plan that clearly outlines how it measures student outcomes.

A high-resolution bound copy of the *Saint Paul Public Schools Best Practices for Tutoring Programs: A Guide to Quality* can be requested by e-mailing tutor@sppsfoundation.org or calling 651-325-4254. A version can also be downloaded in a PDF version at http://sppsfoundation.org/sites/default/files/best_practices_for_tutoring_programs_-_low_res_0.pdf.

As a supplement to the guide, the Saint Paul Public Schools have also collated in-depth handbooks, templates, and examples that programs can use as they implement best-practice strategies.

APPENDIX C

Resources for Engaging Parents in Education

Source: U.S. Department of Education (2007). *Engaging parents in education: Lessons from five parental information and resource centers. Innovations in education.* Washington, DC: WestEd, San Francisco, CA. Retrieved from ERIC database (ED498407), http://eric.ed.gov/.

- Harvard Family Research Project is located in the Harvard Graduate School of Education. It helps policymakers, practitioners, and philanthropic organizations to develop strategies to support more effective educational programs, practices, and policies for all children, particularly disadvantaged children due to poverty and other challenging circumstances. The project also provides featured relevant research and information that the project has collected, analyzed, and synthesized, as well as a link to the Family Involvement Network of Educators, a national network of individuals who are interested in the promotion of partnerships among children's families, educators, and their communities (http://www.hfrp.org).
- Parental Information and Resource Centers (PIRCs) help implement successful and effective parental involvement policies, programs, and activities. These activities lead to improvements in student academic achievement and strengthen partnerships among parents, teachers, principals, administrators, and other school personnel to meet the education needs of children. Section 5563 of the Elementary and Secondary Education Act (ESEA) requires recipients of PIRC grants to serve both rural and urban areas; use at least half their funds to serve areas with

high concentrations of low-income children; and use at least 30 percent of the funds they receive for early childhood parent programs (http://www2.ed.gov/programs/pirc/index.html).

- Parents for Public Schools is a national organization with community-based chapters working in public schools to improve education. The organization accomplishes its mission through strategies and programs that educate, engage, and mobilize parents. The website offers links to all the local chapters that offer a range of services, such as trainings, outreach events, and information on school enrollment. The websites for the national organization and local chapters also include links to a range of other organizations that provide resources for advocacy, training, and many other types of assistance (http://www.parents4publicschools.com).

- The Parent Teacher Association (PTA) is a national nonprofit organization with state and local offices around the nation. The organization is comprised of millions of families, students, teachers, administrators, and business and community leaders devoted to the educational success of children and the promotion of parental involvement in schools. The national website offers a range of resources that includes parent resources, relevant current event articles and stories, and information about training opportunities. The organization also provides a tool to help visitors find their local PTA chapters (http://www.pta.org).

- The Prichard Committee for Academic Excellence is an independent nonprofit education advocacy organization that serves the state of Kentucky. The Prichard Committee initiated the Commonwealth Institute for Parent Leadership (CIPL). The CIPL offers a variety of programs that bring together parents, teachers, community members, and school administrators. These individu-

als are provided with training, information, and experiences that help them work as partners to raise student achievement. CIPL has a well-developed curriculum to help parents understand how the state reform law works; how to build productive partnerships with school staff, parents, and community members; and how to access and use data on student performance both to hold schools accountable and develop programs to improve achievement (http://www.prichardcommittee.org).
- The Right Question Institute makes democracy work better by teaching a strategy that allows individuals to learn to ask better questions and participate more effectively in key decisions that affect them, regardless of their educational, income, or literacy level. The organization website provides materials and publications, information on training sessions and consulting services, and stories of how other organizations and participants have used their services (http://www.rightquestion.org).
- The Southwest Educational Development Laboratory (SEDL) is a nonprofit education research, development, and dissemination organization that works with professionals in schools, districts, states, and service agencies. The SEDL mission is to strengthen connections among research, policy, and practices to improve education for all students. SEDL members believe that improvement of the educational system to meet the needs of all children requires a strong research base that is firmly linked to practice. SEDL partners with educators, administrators, parents, and policymakers to conduct research and development projects that result in strategies and resources to improve teaching and learning. SEDL also helps its partners and clients bridge the gap between research and practice with professional development, technical assistance, and information services tailored to meet their part-

ners' and clients' needs. SEDL's dissemination activities help its partners interpret and apply research findings based on individual contexts and experiences (http://www.sedl.org/welcome.html).

References

Abrar, P. (2013). Pearson completes 100% acquisition of TutorVista, appoints Srikanth Blyer as CEO. *The Economic Times.* Retrieved from http://articles.economictimes.indiatimes.com/2013-02-25/news/37289148_1_tutorvista-krishnan-ganesh-pearson-education-services.

Adler, M. A. (1999). *The America Reads Challenge: An analysis of college students' tutoring.* Ann Arbor: Center for the Improvement of Early Reading Achievement, University of Michigan. Retrieved from ERIC database (ED447413), http://eric.ed.gov/.

Alliance for Excellent Education. (2011). *The high cost of high school dropouts: What the nation pays for inadequate high schools.* Issue Brief. Washington, DC. Retrieved from ERIC database (ED537542), http://eric.ed.gov/.

Anderson, S. B., & S. Ball. (1978). *The profession and practice of program evaluation.* Thousand Oaks, CA: Jossey-Bass. Retrieved from ERIC database (ED175384), http://eric.ed.gov/.

Araya, K. (2012). *Tutoring businesses help fill gap left by education budget cuts.* Retrieved from: http://www.bizjournals.com/sacramento/print-edition/2012/09/28/tutoring-businesses-fill-gap-from-cuts.html?page=all.

Baker, R. S., A. T. Corbett, & K. R. Koedinger. (2004). *Detecting student misuse of intelligent tutoring systems.* Proceedings of the 7th International Conference on Intelligent Tutoring Systems. 531–540. Maceio, Brazil.

Bloom, B. (1984). The 2 sigma problem: The search for methods of group instruction as effective as one-to-one tutoring. *Educational Researcher 13*(6): 4–16.

Bogart, M., & R. Hirshberg. (1993). *A holistic approach to student retention*. Paper presented at the Annual Regional Reading and Study Skills Conference. Retrieved from ERIC database (ED355499), http://eric.ed.gov/.

Bonci, A., E. Mottram, & E. McCoy (2010). *A review of the research evidence underpinning Partners in Literacy*. London: National Trust Literacy. Retrieved from ERIC (ED513441), http://eric.ed.gov/.

Brailsford, A. (1991). *Paired reading: Positive reading practice*. Kelowna, British Columbia: Filmwest Associates. Retrieved from ERIC database (ED345221), http://eric.ed.gov/.

Bridgeland, J. M., J. J. Dilulio, & S.C. Wulsin, Jr. (2008). *Engaged for success: Service-learning as a tool for high school dropout prevention*. Washington, DC. Retrieved from ERIC database (ED503357), http://eric.ed.gov/.

Brooks, J. G., & M. G. Brooks. (1999). *In search of understanding: The case for constructivist classrooms*. Association for Supervision and Curriculum Development, Washington, DC. Retrieved from ERIC database (ED431762), http://eric.ed.gov/.

Brophy, J. E. (1998). *Motivating students to learn*. Boston, MA: McGraw-Hill.

———. (2004). *Motivating students to learn*. 2nd ed. Boston, MA: McGraw-Hill.

———. (2001). Introduction. In J. Brophy (ed.), *Advances in research on teaching 8*, 1–23. Oxford: JA1 Elsevier.

Broward Community College (BCC). (2005). *Does tutoring help? A comparison of Smarthinking-tutored and non-tutored students' grades college-wide*. Fort Lauderdale, FL: Broward Community College. Retrieved from: http://cit.westfield.ma.edu/smarthinking/pdf/smarthinking_proven.pdf.

———. (2005a). *Smarthinking gets results: Students using Smarthinking at Broward Community College have higher pass rates*. Fort Lauderdale, FL: Broward Community College. Retrieved from: file:///C:/Users/Andrea%20%20R/Downloads/SMARTHINKING%20Gets%20Results,%20Broward%20CC%20-(1).pdf.

Bruner, J. S. (1990). *Acts of meaning*. Cambridge, MA: Harvard University Press.

Building Educated Leaders for Life (BELL). (2013). *Building Educated Leaders for Life 2012–2013 afterschool evaluation report*. Retrieved from http://issuu.com/experiencebell/docs/bell_after_school_12-13_evaluation_/1?e=4625325/4833088.

———. (2014). *Building Educated Leaders for Life 2013–2014 afterschool impact report*. Retrieved from: http://issuu.com/experiencebell/docs/about_bell_900b8551b7e94d.

Calfee, J. (2007). Online tutoring and student success in developmental writing courses. *Journal of Applied Research in Community Colleges 15*(1): 77–80. Retrieved from ERIC database (EJ897792), http://eric.ed.gov/.

Carnevale, A. P., N. Smith, & J. Strohl. (2010). *Help wanted: Projections of jobs and education requirements through 2018*. Washington, DC: Georgetown Center on Education and the Workforce. Retrieved from ERIC database (ED524310), http://eric.ed.gov/.

Center for Prevention Research and Development. (2009). *Background research: Tutoring programs*. Champaign, IL: Center for Prevention Research and Development, Institute of Government and Public Affairs, University of Illinois.

Chediak, M. (2005). Online tutoring part of growing trend: Market for web education matures. *The Washington Post*. p. 4. Retrieved from http://www.washingtonpost.com/wp-dyn/content/article/2005/08/15/AR2005081501265.html.

Cohen, P. A., J. A. Kulik, & C. L. C. Kulik. (1982). Educational outcomes of tutoring: A meta-analysis of findings. *American Educational Research Journal 19*(2): 237–248. Retrieved from ERIC database (EJ272101), http://eric.ed.gov/.

Coleman, J. S., E. Q. Campbell, C. J. Hobson, J. McPartland, A. M. Mood, F. D. Weinfeld, & R. L. York. (1966). *Equality of educational opportunity*. Washington, DC: U.S. Government Printing Office.

Common Core State Standards Initiative (CCSSI). (2010). *Standards for English Language Arts & Literacy in History/Social Studies, Science, and Technical Subjects. Council of Chief State School Officers and the National Governors Association Center for Best Practices*. Washington, DC: Authors. Retrieved from http://www.corestandards.org/assets/CCSSI_ELA%20Standards.pdf.

Cooley, C. H. (1902). *Human nature and the social order*. New York, NY: Scribner's.

Cooper, H. (1989). *Homework*. White Plains, NY: Longman.

Crabbé, A. & P. Leroy. (2008). *The handbook of environmental policy evaluation*. London, UK: Earthscan.

Csikszentmihalyi, M. (1990). *Flow: The psychology of optimal experience*. New York: Harper Collins.

Dearing, E., H. Kreider, S. Simpkins, & H. B. Weiss. (2006). Family involvement in school and low-income children's literacy: Longitudinal associations between and within families. *Journal of Educational Psychology 98*(4): 653–664. Retrieved from ERIC database (EJ746472), http://eric.ed.gov/.

DeFazio, T., & A. Deden. (2008). *Highlights of 2007 SMARTHINKING trial at Open Universities Australia*. In Open Universities Australia. Melbourne, Australia.

Dewey, J. (1938). *Experience and education.* New York: Macmillan.

Education Sciences Reform Act of 2002, Pub. L. 107–279, 20 U.S.C. 9501.

Educational Tutorial Services. (2013). *How to get the most from online tutoring.* Retrieved from http://www.educationaltutorialservices.com/category/online-tutoring/.

826 National, Inc. (2013). *826 National: Writing, publishing, tutoring.* Retrieved from http://www.826national.org/.

Eisner, E. W. (1976). Educational connoisseurship and criticism: Their forms and functions in educational evaluation. *Journal of Aesthetic Education 10,* 135–150. Retrieved from ERIC database (EJ156164), http://eric.ed.gov/.

———. (1998). *The enlightened eye: Qualitative inquiry and the enhancement of educational practice.* Upper Saddle River, NJ: Merrill/ Prentice Hall.

———. (2002). *The educational imagination: On the design and evaluation of school programs.* Upper Saddle River, NJ: Merrill/Prentice Hall.

Elementary and Secondary School Act of 1965 (ESEA), Pub. L. 89–10, § 20, 79 Stat. 77.

Epstein, J. L., M. G. Sanders, S. B. Sheldon, B. S. Simon, K. C. Salinas, N. R. Jansorn & F. L. Van Voorhis, C. S. Martin, B. G. Thomas, M. D. Greenfeld, D. J. Hutchins, & K. J. Williams. (2009). *School, family, and community partnerships: Your handbook for action.* 3rd. ed. Thousand Oaks, CA: Corwin Press.

Family Engagement in Education Act of 2013 (S. 1291/H.R. 2662).

Fantuzzo, J., C. McWayne, M. A. Perry, & S. Childs. (2004). Multiple dimensions of family involvement and their relations to behavioral and learning competencies for urban, low-income children. *The School Psychology Review 33*(4): 467–480. Retrieved from ERIC database (EJ683756), http://eric.ed.gov/.

Farnham, A. (2013). *Biggest online tutor bought by Barry Diller's IAC.* Retrieved from: http://abcnews.go.com/Business/tutoring-online-diller-barry-buys/story?id=18155065.

Fitzpatrick, J. L., J. R. Sanders, & B. R. Worthen. (2010). *Program evaluation: Alternative approaches and practical guidelines.* 4th ed. Boston, MA: Pearson Education, Inc.

Flagg, B. N. (1990). *Formative evaluation for educational technologies.* Hillsdale, NJ: Erlbaum.

———. (2013). *Formative evaluation for educational technologies.* New York, NY: Routledge.

Flouri, E., & A. Buchanan. (2004). Early father's and mother's involvement and child's later educational outcomes. *British Journal of Educational Psychology 74*(2): 141–153. Retrieved from ERIC database (EJ695672), http://eric.ed.gov/.

Gall, M. D., J. P. Gall, & W. R. Borg. (2007). *Educational research: An introduction*. 8th ed. Boston: Allyn and Bacon.

Gibbs, S. (2014). *Effective tutoring: Assembling the pieces*. Retrieved from: https://www.mheonline.com/assets/sra_download/EarlyReadingTutor/MoreInfo/TutoringWhitePaper_FNL.pdf.

Glasersfeld, E. (1989). *Constructivism in education*. Oxford, England: Pergamon Press.

Global Industry Analysts, Inc. (2014). *MCP-1597: Private tutoring: A global strategic business report*. Retrieved from: http://www.strategyr.com/pressMCP-1597.asp.

Goodman, J. (2011). New directions with existing resources: Australian and New Zealand libraries as career development hubs. *Australasian Public Libraries and Information Services 24*(1): 39. Retrieved from: http://www.questia.com/library/journal/1G1-252446866/new-directions-with-existing-resources-australian. Used with permission from the Australasian Public Libraries and Information Services.

Gooler, D. D. (1980). Formative evaluation strategies for major instructional development projects. *Journal of Instructional Development 3*(3): 7–11. Retrieved from ERIC database (EJ224132), http://eric.ed.gov/.

Gordon, E. E. (2009). 5 ways to improve tutoring programs. *Phi Delta Kappan 90*(6): 440–445. Retrieved from ERIC database (EJ829696), http://eric.ed.gov/.

Gordon, E. E., R. R. Morgan, J. A. Ponticell, & C. J. O'Malley. (2004). Tutoring solutions for No Child Left Behind: Research, practice, and policy implications. *NASSP Bulletin 88*(638): 59–68. Retrieved from ERIC database (EJ747918), http://eric.ed.gov/.

———. (2007). *The tutoring revolution: Applying research for best practices, policy implications, and student achievement*. R&L Education. Lanham, MD: Rowman & Littlefield Education. Retrieved from ERIC database (ED494127), http://eric.ed.gov/.

Gullickson, A. (2005). *The evaluation center mission*. Kalamazoo: Western Michigan University: The Evaluation Center.

Guyot, W. M. (1978). Summative and formative evaluation. *The Journal of Business Education 54*(3): 127–129.

Hagan, H. (1927). The value of homework as compared with supervised study. Second Yearbook, *Chicago Principals' Club*, 147–149. Chicago: Chicago Principals' Club.

Hammill, D. D., & S. C. Larsen. (2009). *Test of written language-Fourth edition. (TOWL-4)*. Austin, TX—PRO-ED. Retrieved from ERIC database (EJ945204), http://eric.ed.gov/.

Harris, M. (1980). The roles a tutor plays: Effective tutoring techniques. *English Journal* 69(9): 62–65. Retrieved from ERIC database (EJ238443), http://eric.ed.gov/.

Harvard Family Research Project. (2014). *Press kit.* Cambridge, MA: Author. Retrieved from http://www.hfrp.org/hfrp-news/press-kit.

———. (2014). *Out-of-school time program research and evaluation bibliography.* Cambridge, MA: Author. Retrieved from http://www.hfrp.org/out-of-school-time/cost-database-bibliography/bibliography?topic=16.

Henderson, A. T. (1987). *The evidence continues to grow: Parent involvement improves student achievement.* Columbia, MD: National Committee for Citizens in Education. Retrieved from ERIC database (ED315199), http://eric.ed.gov/.

Henderson, A. T., & K. L. Mapp. (2002). *A new wave of evidence: The impact of school, parent, and community connections on student achievement.* National Center for Family and Community Connections with Schools. Austin, TX: Southwest Educational Development Laboratory. Retrieved from ERIC database (ED474521), http://eric.ed.gov/.

Hewett, B. L. (2006). Synchronous online conference-based instruction: A study of whiteboard interactions and student writing. *Computers and Composition* 23(1): 4–31.

Illeris, K. (2002). *The three dimensions of learning.* Roskilde University Press/NIACE, Copenhagen: Leicester.

Instructional Assessment Resources. (2011). *Evaluate programs: Program evaluation process.* Retrieved from https://www.utexas.edu/academic/ctl/assessment/iar/programs/plan/why-process.php.

Invernizzi, M., & M. Ouellette. (2001). *Improving children's reading ability through volunteer reading tutoring programs.* Washington, DC: National Governors Association Center for Best Practices. Retrieved from ERIC database (ED458570), http://eric.ed.gov/.

Jeynes, W. H. (2005). A meta-analysis of the relation of parental involvement to urban elementary school student academic achievement. *Urban Education* 40(3): 237–269. doi: 10.1177/0042085905274540.

Joint Committee on Standards for Educational Evaluation. (1994). *The program evaluation standards.* 2nd ed. Thousand Oaks, CA: Sage Publications, Inc.

———. (2011). *The program evaluation standards.* 3rd ed. Thousand Oaks, CA: Sage Publications, Inc.

Jordan, G. E., C. E. Snow, & M. V. Porche. (2000). Project EASE: The effect of a family literacy project on kindergarten students' early literacy skills. *Reading Research Quarterly* 35(4): 524–546. Retrieved from ERIC database (EJ616175), http://eric.ed.gov/.

Kanuka, H., & T. Anderson. (1998). Online social interchange, discord, and knowledge construction. *Journal of Distance Education 13*(1): 57–74.

Kirkpatrick, D. L. (1959). Techniques for evaluating training programs. *Journal of the American Society of Training Directors (ASTD) 13*(11): 3–9.

Kirkpatrick, D. L., & J. D. Kirkpatrick. (2006). *Evaluating training programs: The four levels.* 3rd ed. San Francisco, CA: Berrett-Koehler Publishers, Inc. Retrieved from ERIC database (ED382790), http://eric.ed.gov/.

Koerner, T. (1991). Restructuring, reform, and the national goals: What do principals think? *NASSP Bulletin 75*(533): 39–49. Retrieved from ERIC database (EJ424346), http://eric.ed.gov/.

Krabbe, J. L., & M. A. Krabbe. (1995). *Tutor training enhanced by knowledge of tutee expectations.* Paper presented at the 19th annual conference of the National Association for Developmental Education, Chicago. Retrieved from ERIC database (ED394414), http://eric.ed.gov/.

Lepper, M. R., & R. W. Chabay. (1988). *Socializing the intelligent tutor: Bringing empathy to computer tutors.* In H. Mandl & A. Lesgold (Eds.), Learning issues for intelligent tutoring systems (pp. 242–257). New York: Springer-Verlag.

Lepper, M. R., & M. Woolverton. (2002). *Improving academic achievement: Impact of psychological factors in education.* Chapter 7: The wisdom of practice: Lessons learned from the study of highly effective tutors. Edited by Aronson, J. Emerald Group Publishing. Retrieved from http://www.eos.ubc.ca/research/cwsei/resources/INSPIRE-Guidelines.pdf.

Lepper, M. R., M. F. Drake, & T. O'Donnell-Johnson. (1997). *Scaffolding techniques of expert human tutors.* In K. Hogan & M. Pressley (eds.), Scaffolding student learning: Instructional approaches and issues (pp. 108–144). Cambridge: Brookline. Retrieved from ERIC database (ED422375), http://eric.ed.gov/.

Lincoln Y. S., & E. G. Guba. (1980). The distinction between merit and worth in evaluation. *Educational Evaluation and Policy Analysis 2,* 61–71. Retrieved from ERIC database (ED183574), http://eric.ed.gov/.

Lockett, C. (1999). *Proceedings of the National Conference of the Center for the Study of Small/Rural Schools 9th.* Memphis, TN.

Machen, S., J. Wilson, & C. Notar. (2005). Parental involvement in the classroom. *Journal of Instructional Psychology 32*(1): 13–16.

Maeroff, G. I. (2003). *A classroom of one: How online learning is changing our schools and colleges.* New York: Palgrave MacMillan. Retrieved from ERIC database (ED478333), http://eric.ed.gov/.

Maine Department of Education. (2013). *Seventh and eighth grade math teachers called to participate in UMaine study.* Retrieved from: http://mainedoenews.net/2013/02/06/seventh-grade-math-teachers-study/.

Mapp, K. L., & P. J. Kuttner. (2013). *Partners in education: A dual capacity-building framework for family-school partnerships.* A publication of SEDL in collaboration with the U.S. Department of Education. Retrieved from: http://www2.ed.gov/documents/family-community/partners-education.pdf.

Marious, S. E., Jr. (2000). Mix and match: The effects of cross-age tutoring on literacy. *Reading Improvement 37*(3): 126–130. Retrieved from ERIC database (EJ616169), http://eric.ed.gov/.

Mathes, P. G., & L. S. Fuchs. (1994). The efficacy of peer tutoring in reading for students with mild disabilities: A best-evidence synthesis. *School Psychology Review 23*(1): 59–80.

Meece, J., & W. McColskey. (2001). *Improving student motivation: A guide for teachers and school improvement teams.* Tallahassee, Florida: SERVE, Publications Department. Retrieved from ERIC database (ED410197), http://eric.ed.gov/.

Mendicino, M., L. Razzaq, & N. T. Heffernan. (2009). A comparison of traditional homework to computer-supported homework. (Report). *Journal of Research on Technology in Education 41*(3): 331–359. Retrieved from ERIC database (EJ835243), http://eric.ed.gov/.

Mitra, S. (2014). Pearson ups stake in TutorVista to own 100%. *Business Standard Ltd.* Retrieved from: http://www.business-standard.com/article/companies/pearson-ups-stake-in-tutorvista-to-own-100-113022400239_1.html.

Moss, M., J. Swartz, D. Obeidallah, G. Stewart, & D. Greene. (2001). *AmeriCorps tutoring outcomes study.* Cambridge, MA: Abt Associates, Inc. Retrieved from ERIC database (ED464348), http://eric.ed.gov/.

National Center for Education Statistics. (2013). U.S. Department of Education. *The condition of education 2013: Undergraduate enrollment.* NCES 2013-037. Retrieved from ERIC database (ED542714), http://eric.ed.gov/.

National Parent Teacher Association (PTA). (2014). *National PTA and Sylvan learning team up to support student success.* Retrieved from http://www.pta.org/about/newsdetail.cfm?ItemNumber=4071.

National Tutoring Association (NTA). (2013). *Code of Ethics.* Retrieved from: http://www.ntatutor.com/code-of-ethics.html.

Nelson-Royes, A. M. (2012). *Transforming early learners into superb readers: Promoting literacy at school, at home, and within the community.* Lanham, MD: Rowman and Littlefield Education.

Nelson-Royes, A. M., & G. L. Reglin. (2011). After-school tutoring for reading achievement and urban middle school students. *Reading Improvement 48*(3): 105–117. Retrieved from ERIC database (EJ955058), http://eric.ed.gov/.

No Child Left Behind Act of 2001, Pub. L. No. 107–110, 115 Stat. 1425 (2002) (20 U.S.C. § 6301 et seq.).

Ohio Department of Education. (2013). *Sample best practices for parent involvement in schools.* Retrieved from http://education.ohio.gov/Topics/Other-Resources/Family-and-Community-Engagement/Getting-Parents-Involved/Sample-Best-Practices-for-Parent-Involvement-in-Sc.

Oldenburg, R. (1989). *The great good place.* New York: Paragon House.

Ormerod, R. (1995). The role of methodologies in systems strategy development: Reflections on experience. In F. Stowell (ed.), *Information systems provision: The contribution of soft systems methodology,* McGraw-Hill, London.

Owens, T. R. (1973). *Educational evaluation by adversary proceeding.* In E. R. House (ed.), School evaluation: The politics and process. Berkeley: McCutchan Publishing.

Parent Teacher Association (PTA) National Standards for Family-School Partnerships. (2009). *National standards for family-school partnerships: What parents, schools, and communities can do together to support student success.* Retrieved from http://www.pta.org/files/National_Standards.pdf.

Pascarella, E. T., & P. T. Terenzini. (1983). Predicting voluntary freshman year persistence/withdrawal behavior in a residential university: A path analytic validation of Tinto's model. *Journal of Educational Psychology 75*(2): 212–226.

Pascarella, E. T., P. T. Terenzini, & L. Wolfe. (1986). Orientation to college and freshman year persistence/withdrawal decisions. *Journal of Higher Education 57*(2): 156–175.

Patton, M. Q. (2001). *Qualitative research and evaluation methods.* 3rd ed. Thousand Oaks, CA: Sage Publications, Inc.

Piaget, J. (1952). *The origins of intelligence in children.* New York: Basic Books.

———. (1970). *The science of education and the psychology of the child.* New York: Grossman.

Pintrich, P. R., & D. Schunk. (2002). *Motivation in education: Theory, research, and applications.* 2nd ed. Upper Saddle River, NJ: Merrill/Prentice-Hall.

Powers, C. E., & B. L. Hewett. (2008). Building online training programs for virtual workplaces. In P. Zemliansky & K. St. Amant (eds.), *Handbook of research on virtual workplaces and the new nature of business practices.* Hershey, PA: Idea Group, Inc.

PR Newswire Association. (2012). Department of Education funds four-year research evaluation of mathematics online tutoring system. *The Free Library*. Retrieved from http://www.thefreelibrary.com/DepartmentofEducationFundsFour-YearResearchEvaluationof-a0328075920.

———. (2014). Online tutoring found to be consistent with best practices of in person tutoring. *The Free Library*. Retrieved from http://www.thefreelibrary.com/Online+Tutoring+found+to+be+Consistent+with+Best+Practices+of+In...-a0363052394.

Rapoport, T., G. Yair, & R. Kahane. (1989). Tutorial relations: The dynamics of social contract and personal trust. *Interchange 20*, 14–26.

Ravitch, D. (2010). *The death and life of the great American school system*. New York: Basic Books, 162–163.

Redding, S., J. Langdon, J. Meyer, & P. Sheley. (2004).*The effects of comprehensive parent engagement on student learning outcomes*. Paper presented at the annual meeting of the American Educational Research Association, San Diego, CA. Retrieved from http://www.adi.org/solidfoundation/resources/Harvard.pdf.

Rekrut, M. D. (1994). Peer and cross-age tutoring: The lessons of research. *Journal of Reading 37*(5): 356–362.

Reinheimer, D., & K. McKenzie. (2011). The impact of tutoring on the academic success of undeclared students. *Journal of College Reading and Learning 41*(2): 22–36. Retrieved from ERIC database (EJ926360), http://eric.ed.gov/.

Reisner, E. R., C. A. Petry, & M. Armitage. (1990). *A review of programs involving college students as tutors or mentors in grades K–12*. Washington, DC: U.S. Department of Education. Retrieved from ERIC database (ED318832), http://eric.ed.gov/.

Rippa, S. A. (1997). *Education in a free society: An American history*. White Plains, NY: Addison Wesley Longman.

Ritter, G. W., J. H. Barnett, G. S. Denny, & G. R. Albin. (2009). The effectiveness of volunteer tutoring programs for elementary and middle school students: A meta-analysis. *Review of Educational Research 79*(1): 3–38. Retrieved from ERIC database (EJ879158), http://eric.ed.gov/.

Roe, M. F., & C. Vukelich. (2001). Understanding the gap between America Reads Program and the tutoring sessions: The nesting of challenges. *Journal of Research in Childhood Education 16*(1): 39–52. Retrieved from ERIC database (EJ643640), http://eric.ed.gov/.

Roskos, K., C. Vukelich, & V. Risko, V. (2001). Reflection and learning to teach reading: A critical review of literacy and general teacher education studies. *Journal of Literacy Research 33*(4): 595–635. Retrieved from ERIC database (EJ650315), http://eric.ed.gov/.

Rubin, D. (1997). *Diagnosis and correction in reading instruction.* 3rd ed. Boston: Allyn & Bacon.

Saint Paul Public Schools Foundation. (2013). *Best practices for tutoring programs: A guide to quality.* 2nd ed. Saint Paul, MN: Greater Twin Cities United Way. Used with permission from the Saint Paul Public Schools Foundation.

Sattes, B. D. (1985). *Parent involvement: A review of the literature* (Report No. 21). Charleston, WV: Appalachia Educational Laboratory.

Schmidt, H. (2011). Communication patterns that define the role of the university-level tutor. *Journal of College Reading and Learning 42*(1): 45–60. Retrieved from ERIC database (EJ961151), http://eric.ed.gov/.

Scriven, M. S. (1973). Goal-free evaluation. In Ernest R. House (ed.), *School evaluation: The politics and process.* Berkeley, CA: McCutchan Publishing Company.

———. (1994). Evaluation as a discipline. *Studies in Educational Evaluation 20*, 147–166.

Shanahan, T., & R. Barr. (1995). Reading recovery: An independent evaluation of the effects of an early instructional intervention for at-risk learners. *Reading Research Quarterly 30*(4): 958–996. Retrieved from ERIC database (EJ511644), http://eric.ed.gov/.

Shaver, A. V., & R. T. Walls. (1998). Effect of Title I parent involvement on student reading and mathematics achievement. *Journal of Research and Development in Education 31*(2): 90–97. Retrieved from ERIC database (EJ561992), http://eric.ed.gov/.

Short, L., M. Hennessy, & J. Campbell. (1996). Tracking the work. In *Family violence: Building a coordinated community response: A guide for communities* (pp. 59–72). Chicago: American Medical Association.

Smarthinking, Inc. (2014). *Smarthinking: The leader in on-demand student support.* Retrieved from http://www.smarthinking.com/about-us/.

Smith, B. (1999). Higher education: The vision [2015]. *Converge Magazine.* Retrieved from http://cgi.stanford.edu/~dept-ctl/tomprof/posting.php?ID=171.

SRI International. (2012). *Department of Education funds four-year research evaluation of mathematics online tutoring system.* Retrieved from: http://www.sri.com/.

Stake, R. E. (1967). The countenance of educational evaluation. *Teachers College Record 68*(7): 523–540.

———. (2001). *Evaluation of testing and criterial thinking in education.* Annual meeting of the American Psychological Association.

State Board of Education Parent and Family Involvement Policy. (2007). Retrieved from https://education.ohio.gov/getattachment/Topics/Other-Resources/

Getting-Involved-with-your-Child-s-Learning/Parent-and-Family-Involvement-Policy-Provides-Guid/Parent-Involvement.pdf.aspx.

States News Service. (2011). *Quote from a Chinese Proverb: A time to be involved, a time to remember.* HighBeam Research. Retrieved from http://en.thinkexist.com/quotes/like/tell_me_and_i-ll_forget-how_me_and_i_may/10546/.

Stufflebeam, D. L., & C. L. S. Coryn. (2013). *Evaluation theory, models, and applications.* 2nd ed. San Francisco, CA: Jossey-Bass.

Stufflebeam, D. L., & A. J. Shinkfield. (2007). *Evaluation theory, models, and applications.* San Francisco, CA: Jossey-Bass.

Sullivan, M. (2011). *Behind America's tutor boom.* MarketWatch Inc. Retrieved from http://www.marketwatch.com/story/behind-americas-tutor-boom-1318016-970246.

Sullivan, P. (2010). Private tutoring booms, parents look at the returns. *The New York Times.* Retrieved from http://www.nytimes.com/2010/08/21/your-money/21wealth.html?pagewanted=all&_r=0.

Swanson, K. L., & M. S. Hertz. (1998). We love to read—A collaborative endeavor to build the foundation for lifelong readers. *Reading Horizons 39*(2): 131–152. Retrieved from ERIC database (EJ579299), http://eric.ed.gov/.

Sweet, A. P., & J. T. Guthrie. (1996). How children's motivations relate to literacy development and instruction (National Reading Research Center). *The Reading Teacher 49*(8): 660–662. Retrieved from ERIC database (EJ527356), http://eric.ed.gov/.

Tapscott, D. (1998). *Growing up digital: The rise of the net generation.* New York: McGraw Hill Companies.

The Times of India. (2011). Pearson buys 76% in TutorVista. Retrieved from: http://www.tutorvista.com/press/mediakitpdf/paper-clips-jan19-2011.pdf.

Thomas, W. P., & V. Collier. (1997). *School effectiveness for language minority students.* Washington, DC: National Clearinghouse for Bilingual Education. Retrieved from ERIC database (ED436087), http://eric.ed.gov/.

Thurston, P. (1978). Revitalizing adversary evaluation: Deep dark deficits or muddled mistaken musings. *Educational Researcher 7*(7): 3–8. Retrieved from ERIC database (EJ186214), http://eric.ed.gov/.

Tinto, V. (1997). Classrooms as communities: Exploring the educational character of student persistence. *The Journal of Higher Education 68*(6): 599–623. Retrieved from ERIC database (EJ555722), http://eric.ed.gov/.

Topping, K. (1998). Effective tutoring in America reads: A reply to Wasik. *The ReadingTeacher 52*(1): 42–50. Retrieved from ERIC database (EJ571645), http://eric.ed.gov/.

Tyler, R. W. (1950). General statement of evaluation. *Journal of Educational Research 35*(4): 492–501.

United Way Worldwide. (2011). *Research supporting: The Education volunteer call to action.* Alexandria, VA. Retrieved from http://unway.3cdn.net/7c37965ebd90788b20_uqm6bfb9y.pdf.

U.S. Department of Education. (1996). *Getting America's students ready for the 21st century: Meeting the technology literacy challenge. A report to the nation on technology and education.* Washington, DC: Department of Education. Retrieved from ERIC database (ED398899), http://eric.ed.gov/.

———. (1997). *Evidence that tutoring works. America reads challenge resource kit.* Washington, DC: Office of the Under Secretary, U.S. Department of Education. Retrieved from: https://jfs.ohio.gov/owd/WorkforceProf/Youth/Docs/WW-tutoring-web.pdf.

———. (2004). *Parental involvement: Title I, Part A. Non-regulatory guidance.* Washington, DC: Department of Education. Retrieved from ERIC database (ED484491), http://eric.ed.gov/.

———. (2007). *Engaging parents in education: Lessons from five parental information and resource centers. Innovations in education.* Washington, DC: WestEd, San Francisco, CA. Retrieved from ERIC database (ED498407), http://eric.ed.gov/.

———. (2012). Institute of Education Sciences. *An efficacy study of online mathematics homework support: An evaluation of the ASSISTments formative assessment and tutoring platform.* Retrieved from: http://ies.ed.gov/funding/grantsearch/details.asp?ID=1273.

Vellutino, F. R., D. M. Scanlon, E. R. Sipay, S. G. Small, A. Pratt, R. Chen, & M. B. Denckla. (1996). Cognitive profiles of difficult-to-remediate and readily remediated poor readers: Early intervention as a vehicle for distinguishing between cognitive and experiential deficits as basic cause of specific reading disability. *Journal of Educational Psychology 88*(4): 601–638. Retrieved from ERIC database (EJ540331), http://eric.ed.gov/.

Vygotsky, L. S. (1962). *Thought and language* (E. Hanfmann & G. Vakar, eds. & trans.). Cambridge, MA: MIT Press.

———. (1978). *Mind in society: The development of higher psychological processes.* Cambridge, MA: Harvard University Press.

Walonoski J., & N. T. Heffernan. (2006). Detection and analysis of off-task gaming behavior in intelligent tutoring systems. In Ikeda, Ashley & Chan (eds.), *Proceedings of the Eighth International Conference on Intelligent Tutoring Systems* (pp. 382–391). Heidelberg, Germany: Springer Berlin.

Wasik, B. A., & R. E. Slavin. (1993). Preventing early reading failure with one-to-one tutoring: A review of five programs. *Reading Research Quarterly 28*(2): 179–200. Retrieved from ERIC database (EJ462260), http://eric.ed.gov/.

Weiss, C. H. (1972). *Evaluation research: Methods for assessing program effectiveness*. Englewood Cliffs, NJ: Prentice Hall.

Weissbord, M. (1973). The OD contract. *OD Practitioner 5*, 1–4.

What Works Clearinghouse. (2008). *Beginning reading: Reading Recovery*. U.S. Department of Education, Institute of Education Sciences. Retrieved from https://readingrecovery.org/images/pdfs/Reading_Recovery/Research_and_Evaluation/wwc_reading_recovery_report_08.pdf.

Wilder Research. (2007). *Evaluation of the East Side Learning Center tutoring program*. St. Paul, MN: J. L. Schultz, & D. Mueller, 11.

Wolf, R. L. (1975). Trial by jury: A new evaluation method. *Phi Delta Kappan 3*(57): 185–187.

Worcester Polytechnic Institute. (2012). *Department of education funds four-year research evaluation of mathematics online tutoring system*. Retrieved from: http://www.wpi.edu/news/20112/srimaine.html .

Yarbrough, D. B., L. M. Shulha, R. K. Hopson, & F. A. Caruthers. (2011). *The program evaluation standards: A guide for evaluators and evaluation users*. 3rd ed. Thousand Oaks, CA: Sage Publications, Inc.

Xu, M., B. Kushner, N. Susan, R. Mudrey-Camino, & R. P. Steiner. (2010). The relationship between parental involvement, self-regulated learning, and reading achievement of fifth graders: A path analysis using the ECLS-K database. *Social Psychology of Education: An International Journal 13*(2): 237–269. Retrieved from ERIC database (EJ885460), http://eric.ed.gov/.

Index

academic achievement, 1–2, 10
Academic Skill Building Program Quality Assessment, 74
Academy for Educational Development, 88
Academy in Athens, 8
accommodation process, 19
accuracy (A) standards, 154–155
Adequate Yearly Progress (AYP), 11
Adler, Martha, 61
adversary evaluation models, 52–53
after-school programs: BELL's principles for, 87; BELL's tutoring and outcomes of, 85–86, 88, 89–90, 91; 826 National tutoring, 80, 82, 84; tutoring programs, x, 3, 25, 26, 28, 61, 86
Alliance for Excellent Education, xiv
America, 8–10
American College Test, 26
American Evaluation Association, 46
analysis: data collection and document, 45; program evaluation process and data, 46–47
Anderson, Scarvia, 30
Anderson, Terry, 17
assessments: ASSISTments' assistance and, 103; tutors' student progress, 66–67, 114
assimilation process, 19
ASSISTments system, 103, 104–105, 106; assistance and assessment integration in, 103; benefits of, 105–106

Australian National Curriculum, 114
AYP. *See* Adequate Yearly Progress

Baker, R. S., 106
Ball, Samuel, 30
BCC. *See* Broward Community College
behaviorism, 16, 145
BELL. *See* Building Educated Leaders for Life
Bell, Derrick A., 85
best practices, vii, 4, 59, 157–161; for parental involvement, 137; parental involvement framework of, 137; SPPS tutoring programs and, 157–161; tutoring programs', 61, 72, 74, 88, 91, 92
Bloom, Benjamin, 143
"A Blueprint for Reform," 12
Bogart, Martha, 28
Bonci, A., 135
Borg, W. R., 12
Brailsford, A., 64
Bridgeland, J. M., 148
Brooks, Jacqueline, 22
Brooks, Martin, 22
Brophy, Jere E., 13–14, 125
Broward Community College (BCC), 100–101, 101, 102
Bruner, Jerome, 17, 20–21
Buchanan, A., 135
budgets, 76

181

Building Educated Leaders for Life (BELL): after-school programs' principles of, 87; after-school tutoring and outcomes of, 85–86, 88, 89–90, 91; literacy and mathematics instruction of, 85, 86, 88, 89; national recognition of, 88; origin and description of, 85–86; strategic partners of, 86; students' underperformance and, 90; tutoring program of, 72, 85–91, 92

Calderon, Larry, 101
Calegari, Nínive, 80
Calfee, Jane, 101
Carter, Andrew Lamar Jr., 85
Center for Evaluation and Assessment (CEA), 35
Center for Prevention Research and Development, 67
Center for Research on Evaluation, Standards, and Student Testing (CRESST), 33–34
Center for Study of Evaluation (CSE), 33
Chabay, Ruth W., 128
Chediak, M., 97–98
Child Trends, 73
CIPL. See Commonwealth Institute for Parent Leadership
classrooms: coordination with teachers and, 67, 114–115; support of teachers and, 82; tutoring freedom of constraint in, 146
Clay, Marie, 70
Code of Ethics, National Tutoring Association, 69–70
cognitivism, 16, 22–23, 128, 145
Cohen, P. A., 64–65, 143
Coleman, J. S., 133–134
Coleman Report. See "Equality of Educational Opportunity"
College Ready grants, 107
Common Core State Standards, xiii–xiv, 86, 103, 119; motivation and, 126; teachers and, 12
Commonwealth Institute for Parent Leadership (CIPL), 163–164
community, 82
companies, 97–98, 116–117, 117–118, 119–121

computers, 108, 110
conferences, 122
Congress, 141
connoisseurship: evaluations and, 48–50; origin and definition of, 48–49
connoisseurship evaluation model, 49
constructivism: active engagement as best in, 17; cognitive form of, 17; founders of, 17; intellectual growth theory in cognitive, 18–19; learning theories and, 16–21, 145; social form of, 17; stakeholders' appreciation by, 23; teaching recommendations for, 22–23; theoretical background and principles of, 17–21
context evaluations, 56
Cooley, C. H., 62–63
cost effectiveness, 95
"Countenance of Educational Evaluation," 32
creativity, 85
CRESST. See Center for Research on Evaluation, Standards, and Student Testing
CSI. See Center for Study of Evaluation
Csikszentmihalyi, Mihaly, 93–94
culture of evaluation: budgets, 76; data collection and, 75–76; recommendations for, 74–76

data collection: culture of evaluation and, 75–76; document analysis for, 45; focus groups and, 45; human subjects in, 45, 46; as improvement tool, 77; indicators and methods for, 44–45; for program evaluation process, 44–46
The Death and Life of the Great American School System (Ravitch), 126
Department of Education, U.S., 64, 102, 103, 106, 121–122, 135, 147
Dewey, John, 17, 18
disabilities, 148–149
drop outs, xiv, 142

education, 10; evaluation role in, 33–36; Internet services for, 98; learning theories of psychology and, 14–15; online tutoring as setting for, 95–108; parental involvement in, 133–134;

programs for special, 2; tutoring and importance of, xiii, 143; tutoring as gold standard in, 2. *See also* instruction; interactive learning; *specific acts and organizations*
Educational Research: An Introduction (Gall, M. D., Gall, J. P., and Borg), 12
Educational Tutorial Services, 96–97
Education Industry Association (EIA), 11–12
Education Resources Information Center (ERIC), 35
Eduventures, 12
Eggers, Dave, 80
EIA. *See* Education Industry Association
826 National: after-school tutoring programs, 80, 82, 84; creativity in programs of, 85; impact results of, 84; model, 81–82; plan priorities for, 83–84; third places of, 81; tutoring program, 72, 80–85, 91, 92; tutoring programs' queried by, ix, x
Eisner, Elliot, 48–50
Elementary and Secondary Education Act (ESEA), 11, 33, 138–139, 139
ELL. *See* English language learners
e-mails, 123
endorsements, 139–140
engagement, 17
English language learners (ELL), 82
enrollments, xiv
epistemology, 15
"Equality of Educational Opportunity" (Coleman Report), 133–134
equilibration process, 19
ERIC. *See* Education Resources Information Center
ESEA. *See* Elementary and Secondary Education Act
essentials, for tutors, 68
evaluation (E) accountability standards, 155
Evaluation Advisory Board, 88
Evaluation Center: mission of, 36; at Western Michigan University, 35–36
evaluations: accountability (E) standard, 155; additional models for, 57–58; benefits of good system for, 79; capabilities of program, 30; CEA completed, 35; connoisseurship and, 48–50; context, 56; culture of, 74–76; decision makers informed by, 32–33; education and role of, 33–36; formative, 39; formative and summative, 39, 40–41; formative progress queries in, 40; goal determinations in, 31; importance and purposes of, 29–33; as improvement tools, 32, 76–77, 146; input, 57; journals specializing in, 36; models and approaches for, 48, 77–80; NCEE supported programs for, 34–35; NCLB proposals for, 36; origins and definition of, 29–30; plan creation for program, 44; plan for, 77–80; process, 57; product, 57; requirements for program, 31–32; resources for, 59; stakeholders and purpose of, 31; standards for, 37–39; summative, 40–41; summative and formative, 39, 40–41; summative progress queries in, 41; types of, 39. *See also* models; program evaluation process

FaceTime, 96
family engagement: Congress' findings on, 141; parental involvement and, 138–139, 147–148
Family Engagement Education Act, 4–5, 125, 148; endorsements for, 139–140; PTA and, 138–142; school fund allowances by, 139
Farnham, A., 121
feasibility (F) standards, 153
federal programs, 27
feedback, 65–66, 103, 107
Fitzpatrick, J. L., 53
Flouri, E., 135
focus groups, 45
formative evaluations, 39
frameworks, philosophical, 16, 27, 145
Fuchs, L. S., 65
funds, 148; ESEA allowance of school, 139; learning theories as basis for, 13; for school improvement items, 139; Title I and SES, 10–11

Gall, J. P., 12

Gall, M. D., 12, 54
Ganesh, Krishnan, 117
Ganesh, Meena, 117
Generation Next, 74
geographical access, Tutoring Australasia's, 116
Gergen, Christopher, 97–98
GIA. *See* Global Industry Analysts
Gibbs, Susan, 61
Glasersfeld, Ernst von, 17
Global Industry Analysts (GIA), 119–121, 144
globalization, 122, 146; of online tutoring, 117–118, 119; private tutoring companies in, 119–121
goal-free evaluation model, 51–52
goals, 51–52; evaluation and determination of, 31; motivation and setting of, 126–127; Tutoring Partnership and, 72–73
gold standard, 2
Goodman, Jack, 108–117
Gordon, E. E., 2, 65, 143
grants, 36, 72, 73, 76, 106–107, 139–140, 162–163
The Great Good Place (Oldenburg), 81
Great Lakes Higher Education Guaranty Corporation, 107
Growing Up Digital: The Rise of the Net Generation (Tapscott), 94–95
guidance, 42–48
Guiding Principles for Evaluators, 46
Gullickson, A., 57
Guthrie, J. T., 129
Guyot, Wally M., 40

Hagan, H., 102–103
Harvard Family Research Project, 59, 162
Harvard University, 85
Heffernan, Neil T., 103, 104–105, 106
Heffernan National Science Foundation, 106
Henderson, Anne T., 134–135
Hewett. B. L., 97–98
Hirshberg, Ruth, 28
history: of early American tutoring programs, 8–10; of tutoring programs, x, xi, 7–10; tutoring programs' origins in, 8–10

homeschooling, 2
homework: mathematics and online tutoring, 102–103, 104–105, 107–108; online tutoring systems for, 107–108; traditional or computerized, 108, 110; Tutoring Australasia and student, 111–112
human subjects, 45, 46

IES. *See* Institute of Education Sciences
improvement tools, 75; data collections as, 77; evaluations as, 32, 76–77, 146; program practice measurements as, 77
India, 118–119
industry, 11–12, 144
input evaluations, 57
INSPIRE: Model for Tutoring Success, 128–129, 130
Institute of Education Sciences (IES), 34, 102
institutions, 4. *See also* international institutions
instruction: BELL's literacy and mathematics, 85, 86, 88, 89; schools' shifts in, 1; scientifically based, 27
integration, social, 28
interactive learning, 4, 93–95
Interdisciplinary Doctor of Philosophy in Evaluation, 36
international institutions: for online tutoring, 108–119; Tutoring Australasia, 108–117; Tutor Vista, 117–119
Internet: cost effectiveness of learning on, 95; educational services, 98
interpersonal relationships, 61–63

Jeynes, William, 136
Johnson, Lyndon B., 33
Joint Committee on Standards for Educational Evaluation, 37, 38, 48; professional standards' categories by, 38–39; Program Evaluation Standards Safety and, 151–155; sponsoring organizations of, 37
Jordan, G. E., 134–135
journals, 36
judicial evaluation model, 52, 53–54

Kanuka, Heather, 17
Kingsbury Center, 66
Kirkpatrick, Donald, 4, 54–55
Kirkpatrick, J. D., 55
Kirkpatrick's four-level evaluation model, 4, 54–55
Koerner, Thomas, 147

Latinos, 86
learning: interactive, 4; Internet, 95; motivation as participation in, 125–127; obstacles, 65; project based, 81; technology and interactive, 93–95
learning theories: constructivism and, 16–21, 145; defining and describing, 12–13; education and psychology's, 14–15; funding basis of, 13; intellectual growth, 18–19; philosophers' tutoring and, 16; philosophical frameworks for, 16, 27, 145; proximal development model in, 20; social context in, 19–20; students' success and, 12–16; tutoring program, x, xi
Lepper, Mark R., 128
libraries, 10, 98, 108–109, 110–111, 122, 149
literacy, 81, 101, 119; mathematics and, 85, 86, 88, 89; motivation and lifelong, 129
logic model: evaluation approaches and, 48, 77–80; facilitating strategies for, 78–79
looking-glass self, 63

Maeroff, G. I., 97–98
Mapp, Karen L., 135
mathematics, 96, 101, 119; literacy and, 85, 86, 88, 89; online tutoring and homework for, 102–103, 104–105, 107–108; research of online tutoring for, 102–108
Mathes, P. G., 65
McColskey, W., 125
McKenzie, K., 144
measurements, program practice, 77
Meece, J., 125
memorization, 18
Mendicino, M., 107, 108
Middle Ages, 8

missions: of Evaluation Center, 36; SRI International, 104; Tutoring Australasia's, 109
models: additional evaluation, 57–58; adversary evaluation, 52–53; connoisseurship evaluation, 49; 826 National, 81–82; evaluation approaches and, 48, 77–80; facilitating strategies for logic, 78–79; goal-free evaluation, 51–52; INSPIRE: Model for Tutoring Success, 128–129, 130; judicial evaluation, 52, 53–54; Kirkpatrick's four-level evaluation, 4, 54–55; objective-based evaluation, 50–51; proximal development, 20; Stufflebeam CIPP evaluation, 4, 56–57
Montessori, Maria, 17
Morency, 127
Moss, M. J., 65
motivation: Common Core State Standards and, 126; factors' importance in, 128–133; learning participation and, 125–127; lifelong literacy and, 129; setting goals and, 126–127; success by parental involvement and, 127; tutoring programs and students', 3, 4–5
motivational factors, 128–133

National Assessment of Educational Progress (NAEP), 51
National Center for Education Evaluation and Regional Assistance (NCEE), 34–35
National Center for Education Statistics, xiv
National Institutes of Health (NIH), 35
National Library of Education, 35
National Parent Association, 4–5, 125
National Science Foundation, 106
National Tutoring Association (NTA), 69–70, 91
NCE. *See* Normal Curve Equivalent
NCEE. *See* National Center for Education Evaluation and Regional Assistance
NCLB. *See* No Child Left Behind Act
Nelson-Royes, Andrea M., x, xi, 64, 104
Net Generation, 4, 93–95
NIH. *See* National Institutes of Health

No Child Left Behind Act (NCLB), xiii, 126; criticism of, 12; evaluation proposals in, 36; SES and Title I funds under, 10–11; tutoring programs and, 10–16
Normal Curve Equivalent (NCE), 89
North America, 118
NTA. *See* National Tutoring Association

Obama, Barack, 12
objective-based evaluation model, 50–51
obstacles, learning, 65
Ohio Department of Education, 137
Oldenburg, Ray, 81
online tutoring, 146; educational setting of, 95–108; Educational Tutorial Services' indications for, 96–97; e-mails for contacting, 123; globalization of, 117–118, 119; higher success rates of, 117, 123; homework assistance systems for, 107–108; India's market and, 118–119; institutions, 4; international institutions for, 108–119; mathematics homework and, 102–103, 104–105, 107–108; new generation companies of, 116–117; older student populations in, 122; research on mathematics, 102–108; Smarthinking provider of, 97–102; students' benefits of, 95–96; tutoring programs for, 3, 25; Tutor Vista and global, 117–118, 119
Open Universities Australia, 117
operating hours, 115
organizations, sponsoring, 37
OST. *See* Out-of-School Time Program Research and Evaluation Bibliography
outcomes, 88
Out-of-School Time (OST) Program Research and Evaluation Bibliography, 90
Owens, Tom, 52–54

Parental Information and Resource Centers (PIRCs), 141–142, 162–163
parental involvement: best practice framework for, 137; best practices for, 137; definition of, 134; in education, 133–134; family engagement and, 138–139, 147–148; research and benefits of, 134–136; resources for engaging, 5, 162–164; significance of, 134–137; success by motivation and, 127; teachers and partnerships in, 142, 146, 147; tutoring programs and, 3, 4–5
Parents, Teachers, and Students Association (PTSA), 140
Parents for Public Schools, 163
Parent Teacher Association (PTA), 138–142, 163
Patton, Michael, 31
payment fees, 115
Pearson company, 97–98, 117–118
Phalen, Earl Martin, 85
philosophers, 16
philosophical beliefs, 15–16
Piaget, Jean, 17, 18–19, 20
Pines, Steve, 11–12
Pintrich, P. R., 125–126
PIRCs. *See* Parental Information and Resource Centers
Powers, C. E., 97–98
Prepare2Nspire, 106
Prichard Committee for Academic Excellence, 163
private global tutoring companies, 119–121
private tutoring, 144
process evaluation, 57
product evaluations, 57
professional standards, 38–39
program evaluation process, 42–48, 77; analysis of data in, 46–47; conclusions and recommendations in, 47; context description in, 42; creation of evaluation plan in, 44; data collection for, 44–46; determination of purpose in, 43; identification of intended uses in, 43–44; program context description in, 42; reporting, 47–48; resources and, 45–46; stakeholder identification and, 42–43; suggested steps for guidance in, 42–48
The Program Evaluation Standards: A Guide for Evaluators and Evaluation Users, 151
Program Evaluation Standards Safety, 151–155

Program Evaluation Standards Statements, 39
program practice measurements, 77
project based learning, 81
propriety (P) standards, 153–154
proximal development model, 20
psychology, 14–15
PTA. *See* Parent Teacher Association
PTSA. *See* Parents, Teachers, and Students Association

Rapoport, T., 7
Ravitch, Diane, 126, 129
Reading Recovery (RR), 4, 70–72, 92
Regional Educational Laboratory Program, 34–35
Reglin, G. L., 64, 104
Reinheimer, D., 144
Reisner, E. R., 64
relationships. *See* interpersonal relationships
remedial programs, 2
research, 143–144; of online tutoring for mathematics, 102–108; parental involvement's benefits, 134–136; SRI International, 102–108; on successful tutoring programs, 71–72, 117, 128, 149; teachers and intervention, 13–14, 14; tutoring program performance, 67; tutoring program usage, 2; University of Maine, 102–108; of WPI, 102–108
resources: for choosing evaluation methods, 59; for evaluation results, 59; for parental involvement, 5, 162–164; program evaluation process and, 45–46
Richards, Gerald, xi
The Right Question Institute, 164
Rippa, S. Alexander, 8–9
risk, 144
Ritter, G. W., 143–144
Roskos, K., 66
RR. *See* Reading Recovery

Saint Paul Public Schools (SPPS) Foundation: best practices for tutoring programs and, 157–161; description and background of, 72; student success commitment of, 79–80; tutoring program, 72–80, 91, 92

Sandler, Michael, 12
SAT. *See* Scholastic Aptitude Test
Sattes, Beth, 134
schemas: accommodation process in, 19; assimilation process in, 19; equilibration process in, 19
Schmidt, H., 62
Scholastic Aptitude Test (SAT), ix, 26
schools: home, 2; instructional shifts in, 1; items for improvement fund usage of, 139; philosophical belief basis of, 15–16. *See also* after-school programs; Saint Paul Public Schools Foundation
Schunk, D., 125–126
Science, Technology, Engineering, and Mathematics (STEM), 106
scientifically based instruction, 27
Scriven, Michael S., 32–33, 51–52
SEDL. *See* Southwest Educational Development Laboratory
service provisions, Smarthinking's, 100
SES. *See* supplementary educational services
Shaver, A. V., 134–135
SIF. *See* Social Innovation Fund
Skype, 96
Slavin, R. E., 65
Smarthinking, Incorporated: effectiveness of, 101; online tutoring provider, 97–102; service provisions of, 100; tutorial workforce of, 98–99
Smith, Burck, 97–98
Social Innovation Fund (SIF), 73, 74
social integration, 28
Socrates, 8, 17
Southwest Educational Development Laboratory (SEDL), 164
special education programs, 2
sponsors, 37
SPPS. *See* Saint Paul Public Schools Foundation
SRI International: missions of, 104; research of, 102–108
Stake, Robert E., 32
stakeholders: constructivism and appreciation of, 23; evaluation's purpose and, 31; program evaluation process and, 42–43; tutoring program and questions of, 3; tutoring programs

and, x–xi
standards: accuracy (A), 154–155; evaluation (E) accountability, 155; feasibility (F), 153; professional, 38–39; propriety (P), 153–154; utility (U), 152. *See also* Common Core State Standards
statistics, xiv
STEM. *See* Science, Technology, Engineering, and Mathematics
students: BELL's underperforming, 90; drop out statistics of, xiv; learning theories and success of, 12–16; Net Generation and interactivity of, 94; online tutoring benefits for, 95–96; online tutoring of older population, 122; at risk of failure, 144; SPPS success commitment to, 79–80; technology bombardment of, 95; tutoring and disabled, 148–149; Tutoring Australasia and attitudes of, 115–116; Tutoring Australasia homework assistance and, 111–112; tutoring programs' motivation of, 3, 4–5; tutoring programs' optimization and, x; tutors as beneficial to, ix–x, x, xiv–xv; tutors' individualized attention to, 63; tutors' progress assessment of, 66–67, 114; Tutor Vista offerings to, 119
Stufflebeam, Daniel L., 56–57
Stufflebeam CIPP evaluation model, 4; context, input, process, and product in, 56–57; development and description of, 56–57
Sullivan, M., 2
summative evaluations, 39, 40–41
supplementary educational services (SES), 10–11
Sylvan, 138
Sylvan Insight Assessment, 138

TAFEs. *See* Technical and Further Education [vocational] institutions
Tapscott, Don, 94–95
teachers: Common Core State Standards and, 12; constructivism recommendations for, 22–23; coordination with classroom and, 67, 114–115; intervention research and, 13–14, 14; parental involvement and partnerships with, 142, 146, 147; support of classrooms and, 82
Teachers of English to Speakers of Other Languages (TESOL), 140
Technical and Further Education [vocational] institutions (TAFEs), 111–112
"Technological Literacy: A National Priority," 121–122
technology, 121, 146; of interactive learning, 4; interactive learning and, 93–95; students' bombardment of, 95; Tutoring Australasia's online, 114; whiteboard, 99–100, 118, 122
TESOL. *See* Teachers of English to Speakers of Other Languages
"The Test of Written Language-Fourth Edition" (TOWL-4), 83
theories. *See* learning theories
third places, of 826 National, 81
Title I funds, 10–11
tools. *See* improvement tools
TOWL-4. *See* "The Test of Written Language-Fourth Edition"
tradition, 108, 110
training: tutors' feedback and intensive, 65–66; tutors with minimal, 66
Tutor Code of Ethics, 69–70, 91
tutoring, private, 144
Tutoring Australasia (core service, Yourtutor): benefits and availability of, 109; description and founding of, 108–109; geographical access to, 116; Goodman and queries regarding, 109–117; international institutions, 108–117; libraries and, 108–109, 110–111; mission of, 109; online technologies of, 114; operating hours of, 115; payment fees and, 115; quality consistency and, 113; student homework assistance and, 111–112; students' attitudes about, 115–116; tutors and, 112–114; Yourtutor as core service of, 108, 109
tutoring companies, 119–121
tutoring formats, 25–27, 28, 145
tutoring industry: capitalization of, 11–12; estimated size of, 12

Tutoring Partnership for Academic Excellence (Tutoring Partnership), 72–73
tutoring programs: academic achievement strategy of, 1–2, 10; accessibility of, 10; after-school, x, 3, 25, 26, 28, 61, 86; BELL's, 72, 85–91, 92; BELL's after-school, 85–86, 87, 88, 89–90, 91; benefits of, 24; best practices, 61, 72, 74, 88, 91, 92, 157–161; cognitivism empowered by, 22–23, 128; consistency for successful, 64–65; cross-age, 25; definition and types of, 2, 7–8; disabled students and, 148–149; early America's history of, 8–10; education and importance of, xiii, 143; effective components of, 63–65; 826 National, 72, 80–85, 91, 92; 826 National after-school, 80, 82, 84; 826 National's queries about, ix, x; establishing, 3; formats of, 25–27, 28, 145; freedom of classroom constraint by, 146; as gold standard in education, 2; history of, x, xi, 7–10; home-based, 25; intensity for successful, 64–65; interpersonal relationships and, 61–63; in Middle Ages, 8; NCLB and, 10–16; online, 3, 25; online institutions for, 4; origins and history of, 8–10; parental involvement vital in, 3, 4–5; purpose and benefits of, 23–24; research and usage of, 2; researches and successful, 71–72, 117, 128, 149; research on performance of, 67; RR, 4, 70–72, 92; significant role of, 149; social integration fostered by, 28; SPPS Foundation's, 72–80, 91, 92, 157–161; stakeholders and, x–xi; stakeholders' questions of, 3; structure for successful, 64–65; students' motivation and, 3, 4–5; successful, 61–62, 63–65, 92, 123; theory of, x, xi; tutor and student optimization in, x; usage of diagnostic/developmental, 65. *See also* after-school programs; online tutoring
The Tutoring Revolution: Applying Research for Best Practices, Policy Implications, and Student Achievement (Gordon), 143

tutors: assessment of student progress by, 66–67, 114; as beneficial to students, ix–x, x, xiv–xv; essentials for, 68; INSPIRE model for success of, 128–129, 130; intensive training and feedback for, 65–66; minimally trained, 66; need for, 144–145; role of successful, 61–62; Smarthinking's workforce of, 98–99; students' individualized attention of, 63; Tutoring Australasia and, 112–114; tutoring programs' optimization and, x
Tutor Vista: description and founding of, 117–118; global online tutoring and, 117–118, 119; international institutions, 117–119; North America as primary engagement of, 118; Pearson company's takeover of, 117–118; student offerings of, 119
"The 2 Sigma Problem," 143
Tyler, Ralph, 50–51

University of California Los Angeles (UCLA), 33, 34
University of Maine, 102–108
University of Minnesota STEM Education Center, 107
utility (U) standards, 152

video conferencing, 122
Voice over Internet Protocol (VoIP), 101, 118
volunteers, 82
Vygotsky, Lev S., 17, 20

Wall, R. T., 134–135
Walonoski, J., 106
Wasik, B. A., 65
Weikart Center for Youth Program Quality, 73–74
Weiss, C. H., 60
Weissbord, M., 60
Western Michigan University, 35–36
What Works Clearinghouse (WWC), 35, 71
whiteboards, 99–100, 118, 122
White House, 148
Whitney, Eli, 10
Wilder Research, 59

W. K. Kellogg Foundation, 148
Wolf, Robert, 52–54
Worcester Polytechnic Institute (WPI), 102–108
WWC. *See* What Works Clearinghouse

Xu, M., 135

Yourtutor. *See* Tutoring Australasia (core service, Yourtutor)
Youth Program Quality Assessment (YPQA), 73–74

About the Author

Andrea M. Nelson-Royes, EdD, is an educational researcher, and author of *Transforming Early Learners into Superb Readers: Promoting Literacy at School, at Home, and within the Community* and *Success in School and Career: Common Core Standards in Language Arts K–5*. Her articles have appeared in the *Reading Improvement Journal* and *Illinois Schools Journal*. Nelson-Royes holds a doctoral degree in educational and organizational leadership from Nova Southeastern University in Florida. She lives in the southeastern United States with her family. Please visit her website at www.andreanelsonroyes.com.

www.ingramcontent.com/pod-product-compliance
Lightning Source LLC
Chambersburg PA
CBHW070724020526
44116CB00031B/1697